The New York Times
BRIDGE SERIES

DOUBLES
AND
REDOUBLES

The New York Times
BRIDGE SERIES

DOUBLES
AND
REDOUBLES

ALAN TRUSCOTT

Times
BOOKS

To thousands of readers who have
contributed interesting deals for the
New York Times bridge column

Library of Congress Cataloging-in-Publication Data
Truscott, Alan F.
The New York times bridge series.
1. Contract bridge—Doubles.
2. Contract bridge—Collections of games.
I. Title.
GV1282.43.T78   1987   795.41′58   86-14467
ISBN 0-812-91628-X

Manufactured in the United States of America
9 8 7 6 5 4 3 2
First Edition

BOOK DESIGN: BARBARA MARKS

CONTENTS

9: FICTION 109

10: THE HUMAN FACTOR 123

11: WEIRD AND WONDERFUL 139

INTRODUCTION

This book continues the series of selected *New York Times* columns that began with *Grand Slams*. Here all the deals feature a double (except one that nearly did) and a handful show a redouble. As this is not intended to be a technical textbook, the reader will not learn directly about penalty doubles, takeout doubles, lead-directing doubles, negative doubles, or even the exotic striped-tailed ape double, although most of these will appear in some guise. The first one third of the book is largely technical, but then we stray into the byways of bridge. The intention is to entertain, and if the reader is educated that is incidental.

The columns have been slightly modified to exclude contemporary references that are now meaningless. In some cases this may have introduced a minor anachronism.

I had always supposed that preparing a collection of columns would be a trivial exercise, not to be compared with the labor needed to produce a book with new material. I find I was wrong. In the time that was consumed in inspecting, comparing, and selecting from some eight thousand columns, I believe I could have written two books. Most of this work was done by Dorothy Hayden Truscott with some help from Phillip Alder. I am grateful to them both and to Terrence Garrigan for his eagle-eyed survey of the manuscript.

REDOUBLES

Redoubles are everyday currency at the bridge table when one is en route to some other contract. There is the redouble of a takeout double, to show that the opponents may be in trouble. There is the redouble to show second-round control when a cue-bid is doubled. These virtually never end the bidding.

The SOS redouble following a penalty double is a scream for help that is occasionally ignored. The redouble when a conventional bid has been doubled suggests a final contract, a suggestion that is spurned more often than it should be. We have an example of each.

At a high level the redouble may be, as in our third example, a tactical gamble aimed at scaring the opponents into an unwise retreat. Or it may be an attempt to take advantage of the mathematics of the scoring table, which tend to favor the redoubler. The second of our two examples shows outstanding imagination by a brilliant young black player who died young.

Redoubled contracts, while dramatic, are very rare in real life and almost as rare in bridge columns. We start with them, thus reversing the batting order suggested by the title.

CANADIANS ON THIN ICE

The Canadian experts Eric Murray and Sam Kehela of Toronto are recognized as one of the very best pairs in the world. In a world championship match against France, they skated on some very thin ice, but fine play turned a likely disaster into a profit.

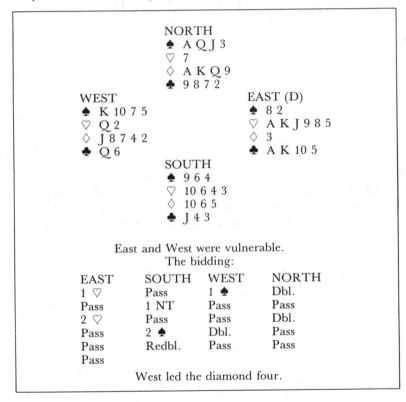

NORTH
♠ A Q J 3
♡ 7
♢ A K Q 9
♣ 9 8 7 2

WEST
♠ K 10 7 5
♡ Q 2
♢ J 8 7 4 2
♣ Q 6

EAST (D)
♠ 8 2
♡ A K J 9 8 5
♢ 3
♣ A K 10 5

SOUTH
♠ 9 6 4
♡ 10 6 4 3
♢ 10 6 5
♣ J 4 3

East and West were vulnerable.
The bidding:

EAST	SOUTH	WEST	NORTH
1 ♡	Pass	1 ♠	Dbl.
Pass	1 NT	Pass	Pass
2 ♡	Pass	Pass	Dbl.
Pass	2 ♠	Dbl.	Pass
Pass	Redbl.	Pass	Pass
Pass			

West led the diamond four.

The development of the auction must have caused Kehela, as South, to feel progressively more gloomy. First he was reduced to bidding one notrump, which suggested a little high-card strength, rather than bidding a three-card suit at the level of two. When he seemed out of trouble after East had rebid two hearts, North refused to be silenced and doubled again.

This time Kehela tried two spades as a first step toward finding a playable contract. However, when he made an SOS redouble, in the expectation of finding a safe landing place in a minor suit at the level of three, Murray chose, wisely as it turned out, to let his partner struggle in this unlikely contract.

West led the diamond four and Kehela could hardly afford to duck in dummy, a play that would have given him an important entry to his own hand. He won with the ace and led the heart seven. East in his turn could not take the risk of ducking, especially as South had bid one notrump. He put up the king and cashed his two club winners, felling his partner's queen in the process. He gave his partner a club ruff and got a diamond ruff in return. The position was then this:

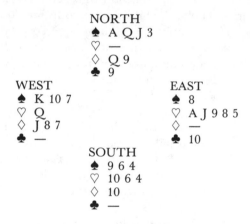

```
                    NORTH
                    ♠ A Q J 3
                    ♡ —
                    ◊ Q 9
                    ♣ 9
     WEST                          EAST
     ♠ K 10 7                      ♠ 8
     ♡ Q                           ♡ A J 9 8 5
     ◊ J 8 7                       ◊ —
     ♣ —                           ♣ 10
                    SOUTH
                    ♠ 9 6 4
                    ♡ 10 6 4
                    ◊ 10
                    ♣ —
```

East led the club ten, no doubt hoping that South would ruff, after which an overruff by West would lead to another diamond ruff by East. But South made a fine play by discarding his diamond ten on the club ten. West discarded the heart queen and East played the heart jack, which dummy ruffed.

South was able to make the remaining tricks. He ruffed the diamond nine in his own hand, finessed the spade queen, and ruffed dummy's diamond queen, scoring dummy's ace–jack of trumps at the finish.

For down one, in the replay East–West made four hearts.

June 4, 1967

OUTNUMBERED BUT VICTORIOUS

Perhaps the most important basic rule of bidding is that eight cards of a suit shared by a partnership constitute a satisfactory trump suit, while fewer do not. Nine times out of ten, if a game is to be attempted it should be in three notrump, unless an eight-card major suit fit can be discovered.

Most of the exceptions arise when there is no eight-card fit, with one suit too weak to permit notrump play. To play in a six-one fit is common enough, while a five-two fit may be best if the suit is strong, missing only one high honor. To play in a four-three fit is a more precarious enterprise, but it may be tried occasionally in a major-suit game contract. The suit should be strong, and it is also important that the three-card trump length should be in the same hand as the shortage in the opponents' suit.

To play with only six trumps in the two hands is usually a sign that the bidding has failed, especially if the six cards are split three–three or four–two. But there is an occasional hand in which a four-two fit is the only road to success, and in the deal shown, played in the expert game at the Cavendish Club, South played in a two-four fit with remarkable success.

Although three notrump can be made as the cards lie, some luck is required and it is not likely to be bid. Left in peace, North and South, Charles Coon and Dorothy Hayden, respectively, would probably stop in two notrump after this auction:

NORTH	SOUTH
1 NT	2 ♣
2 ♡	2 NT
Pass	

South has not quite enough strength to venture three notrump, and North cannot continue to game without reserve strength for his opening bid.

West's double of two clubs was a slightly indiscreet attempt to ask for a club lead against notrump, and it was severely punished. North's redouble showed that he was prepared to play in two clubs, and South made a good decision by passing.

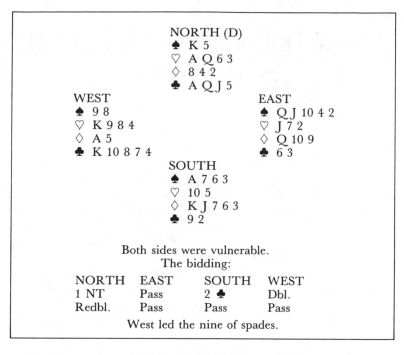

NORTH (D)
♠ K 5
♡ A Q 6 3
◇ 8 4 2
♣ A Q J 5

WEST
♠ 9 8
♡ K 9 8 4
◇ A 5
♣ K 10 8 7 4

EAST
♠ Q J 10 4 2
♡ J 7 2
◇ Q 10 9
♣ 6 3

SOUTH
♠ A 7 6 3
♡ 10 5
◇ K J 7 6 3
♣ 9 2

Both sides were vulnerable.
The bidding:

NORTH	EAST	SOUTH	WEST
1 NT	Pass	2 ♣	Dbl.
Redbl.	Pass	Pass	Pass

West led the nine of spades.

South won the spade lead with the ace and finessed the heart queen successfully. She cashed the heart ace, ruffed a heart, and re-entered dummy with the spade king. Dummy's last heart was ruffed by East with the club six and it was overruffed with the nine. A low spade was led, and West ruffed with the club seven to prevent a ruff by dummy with the five.

Dummy overruffed with the jack, and the diamond jack was finessed, forcing the ace. South had seven tricks in the bag, and had no difficulty making the diamond king and two more trump tricks for a total of ten. The total score was 1,510 points, including two redoubled vulnerable overtricks.

JUNE 24, 1964

ANGRY DOUBLE + WRONG LEAD = DISASTER

Redoubled contracts are very rare when the standard of play is high. When they do occur, an imprudent double is usually to blame. Delicate situations can arise in a high-level competitive auction, when the redoubler has to consider the possibility that his opponents will escape into a contract of their own.

The diagramed deal, illustrating this point, was played in Houston in a rubber bridge game. West felt insulted when his opponents galloped into six hearts, and doubled on the strength of his black-suit winners.

North was not at all sure that six hearts would make, but his redouble was a good tactical gamble. It stood to gain 360, as against a loss of 200 if the result was one down, and there was a chance that East–West would escape into six spades, a contract North knew would be heavily defeated.

The redouble would have been quite unsound if North's prospects in hearts had been better and his prospects against spades had been worse.

West's opening lead of the club king was natural enough, but it turned out disastrously. Milton Freedman of Houston, sitting South, ruffed the opening lead and cashed the heart king. One round of hearts was just enough, and not too much. He cashed the ace and king of diamonds, expecting to be able to establish his fifth diamond by ruffing.

West's discard on the second round of diamonds was most revealing. It was clear that he had no more red cards, so South led his singleton spade and West found himself endplayed. Whatever he did, one of dummy's black queens would be established and South could cross-ruff the remaining tricks.

The contract was made and West was unhappy. He became more unhappy when he realized that he could have led a high spade or one of his singletons to defeat the contract.

NOVEMBER 10, 1967

NORTH (D)
♠ Q 10 9 4
♡ A 9 5
♦ 8 2
♣ Q 9 6 2

WEST
♠ A K J 5 3
♡ 6
♦ 5
♣ A K J 8 4 3

EAST
♠ 8 7 2
♡ J 3
♦ Q J 9 7 4
♣ 10 7 5

SOUTH
♠ 6
♡ K Q 10 8 7 4 2
♦ A K 10 6 3
♣ —

Both sides were vulnerable.
The bidding:

NORTH	EAST	SOUTH	WEST
Pass	Pass	2 ♡	2 ♠
3 ♡	Pass	6 ♡	Dbl.
Redbl.	Pass	Pass	Pass

West led the club king.

CAN YOU MAKE THIS CONTRACT?

The Cavendish in New York City has a good claim to be the world's most famous bridge club. It is crowded with experts who play rubber bridge there when they are not winning national titles. There are also many talented players who confine themselves to club bridge. One of them is Dr. David Dove, who sat South on the diagramed deal and found himself in three notrump redoubled after a lively auction.

West's one heart overcall was a slight underbid, but he could not jump to two hearts, which would be the general choice on standard methods, because his side was using pre-emptive jump overcalls in the modern fashion.

North's first redouble, which caused East to flee in terror to two hearts, was fully justified, but the final redouble was over-optimistic.

The reader should try to make up his mind before reading on whether three notrump should succeed after a heart lead. The key to the hand is West's play to the first spade trick.

After winning the first trick with the heart jack, South led a spade and West put up the ace. Unwilling to give South a trick by leading a second heart or a club, West returned the spade queen. South permitted this to hold and West was headed for more trouble.

He led his singleton diamond, at which point South could count nine tricks: three spades, four diamonds, one heart, and one club. When he had taken his spade and diamond tricks he was reduced to the heart king and ace–ten of clubs. West had to keep the heart ace and the guarded club king, so he was thrown in with a heart lead and forced to lead a club, giving declarer an extra trick with the club queen.

West made a fatal error by playing his spade ace. If he had played the spade queen at the second trick, the declarer would have been defeated: If North had won with the king, the stage would have been set for East to win the third round of spades with his jack and to lead a heart through South.

If South permitted the spade queen to win at this stage, West would simply establish hearts while he still held the spade ace as

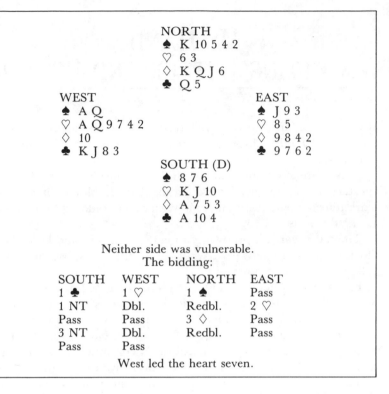

NORTH
♠ K 10 5 4 2
♡ 6 3
♦ K Q J 6
♣ Q 5

WEST
♠ A Q
♡ A Q 9 7 4 2
♦ 10
♣ K J 8 3

EAST
♠ J 9 3
♡ 8 5
♦ 9 8 4 2
♣ 9 7 6 2

SOUTH (D)
♠ 8 7 6
♡ K J 10
♦ A 7 5 3
♣ A 10 4

Neither side was vulnerable.
The bidding:

SOUTH	WEST	NORTH	EAST
1 ♣	1 ♡	1 ♠	Pass
1 NT	Dbl.	Redbl.	2 ♡
Pass	Pass	3 ♦	Pass
3 NT	Dbl.	Redbl.	Pass
Pass	Pass		

West led the heart seven.

an entry. The best South can do is to win the spade king, cash one diamond trick, and lead a spade.

West wins with the spade ace and leads a club, not a heart. Careful defense then wins out. West must keep all his clubs and, to avoid a throw-in, must be able to give East the lead on the fourth round of clubs.

Notice that if South cashes more than one diamond trick after winning the spade king, West can make a brilliant discard of the spade ace.

An opening lead of a club defeats the contract with less difficulty, but West had no reason to make such a choice.

APRIL 27, 1965

MY HAND
IS GETTING BETTER AND BETTER

If you are long in your partner's suit and short in the opponents', you should tend to bid, but if the contrary is true you should tend to defend.

This is an acceptable general guideline, but there can be some spectacular exceptions. The diagramed deal, played in a New York tournament, featured some remarkable bidding by the late Larry Edwards.

The four-heart bid, showing a long, strong suit and little else, did not appeal to Edwards, who sat North, but subsequent developments excited him.

East's takeout double and West's four-spade bid suggested that South held at most a singleton, so the prospects in hearts looked good. Edwards raised to five hearts, a rare action with a void, and thought again when East bid five spades. Now it seemed that South was void in spades, so Edwards continued to six hearts and showed the courage of his convictions by redoubling.

This may well be the first time in the history of the game that a player bid a suit once and then heard his partner not only raise twice with a void but also redouble.

East may have nourished a faint hope that his double would be interpreted as Lightner, asking for an unusual lead. But West did not even consider a diamond lead. The bidding gave no hint that his partner was void in that department, and the double sounded like a penalty action against opponents who were sacrificing.

A spade was led, and the South player, Michael Radin, inspected the dummy in astonishment. When he got over the shock of finding a paucity of trumps he had no trouble in making the redoubled slam by driving out the heart ace and then drawing trumps.

DECEMBER 17, 1985

NORTH
♠ J 8 6 4
♡ —
♢ A K J 9 4 3
♣ A 9 2

WEST
♠ Q 7 3 2
♡ 9 8 6
♢ Q 6
♣ 10 8 7 4

EAST
♠ A K 10 9 5
♡ A 7 2
♢ —
♣ K Q J 6 5

SOUTH (D)
♠ —
♡ K Q J 10 5 4 3
♢ 10 8 7 5 2
♣ 3

North and South were vulnerable.
The bidding:

SOUTH	WEST	NORTH	EAST
4 ♡	Pass	Pass	Dbl.
Pass	4 ♠	5 ♡	5 ♠
Pass	Pass	6 ♡	Dbl.
Pass	Pass	Redbl.	Pass
Pass	Pass		

West led the spade two.

2

LIGHTNER

M ore than half a century ago the late Theodore Lightner thought of a special meaning for a slam double: Make an unusual lead, partner. Unfortunately, the first practical test generated a disaster and his partner, Ely Culbertson, firmly refused to have anything more to do with it.

This was unfortunate for, as experts have recognized ever since, the Lightner double has everything to recommend it: It can swing thousands of points by defeating a contract that would otherwise make, and it can prevent partners from making foolish doubles on the strength of a couple of aces or general honor strength.

But Culbertson's experience is far from unique. The Lightner Slam Double, undoubtedly a success in the long run, is admittedly accident-prone in the short run. In the first deal in this group, West ignores a Lightner double with some excuse: His partner had made a string of lead-directing doubles pointing in different directions. On the second deal West respected his partner's Lightner double and wished he had not. On the third deal, reported by a world-famous tournament director, the lead is on target but the defense gets the worst of it in the long run. On the fourth deal the Lightner lead proves to be an accidental brilliancy for quite the wrong reason. And finally, a famous player sees reason to avoid a Lightner, and his partner reads the situation correctly. For a remarkable psychic Lightner the reader is referred to *Grand Slams*, the first book in this series.

PLENTY OF LEAD DIRECTION BUT STILL WRONG LEAD

The merits of leading "top-of-nothing" from a worthless three-card suit are often debated. Some experts lead the bottom card in this situation, some the middle card, and some vary their tactics, leaving partner and opponents with some guessing to do.

A danger of leading top-of-nothing is that the top card may turn out to be a valuable asset, and squandering it on the first trick can ruin the defense. This point was brought home to West on the diagramed deal played at the New York Insurance Bridge Club. It was reported by Nino Harari, who held the South cards.

East set a world record by making three, and perhaps four, lead-directing doubles in one hand. He asked for a spade lead by doubling three spades. Next he asked for a heart lead by doubling the five-heart response to Blackwood. Then when North bid six diamonds to show possession of one king, East doubled to ask for a diamond lead.

And finally he doubled seven notrump. This was no doubt an expression of outrage at the impertinence of North–South in contracting for a grand slam in the face of the previous doubles, but could be construed as a Lightner double to ask for an unusual lead. As East had already asked for spades, hearts, and diamonds, the unusual lead would have to be clubs.

West may have been confused by his partner's instructions relating to the opening lead. He decided to respect the original double of spades and put the spade nine on the table. It was not easy for him to appreciate that this was a valuable card, but so it proved. Any other lead would have served to defeat the slam.

The declarer had no illusions about the position of the spade king. He won with the ace in dummy, cashed the club queen, and confidently finessed in hearts. He cashed the heart ace and followed with all his club winners.

As the opening lead had left East with the task of keeping the winning spade, a squeeze developed. Dummy came down to the ace–king–ten of diamonds, and East could not keep three diamonds as well as the winning spade.

When the distressing effect of West's opening lead had been

```
                    NORTH
                    ♠ A Q 4
                    ♡ 9 7
                    ◇ A K 10 7 6 4 3
                    ♣ Q
WEST                                        EAST
♠ 9 3 2                                     ♠ K J 10 6
♡ 8 6 5 4 2                                 ♡ K J 10 3
◇ 2                                         ◇ Q J 9 8
♣ 9 7 6 3                                   ♣ 4
                    SOUTH (D)
                    ♠ 8 7 5
                    ♡ A Q
                    ◇ 5
                    ♣ A K J 10 8 5 2
```

Neither side was vulnerable.
The bidding:

SOUTH	WEST	NORTH	EAST
1 ♣	Pass	2 ◇	Pass
3 ♣	Pass	3 ♠	Dbl.
4 NT	Pass	5 ♡	Dbl.
5 NT	Pass	6 ◇	Dbl.
7 NT	Pass	Pass	Dbl.

West led the spade nine.

examined in the postmortem, East suggested that South had been lucky in finding the heart king well placed.

"Not at all," rejoined South. "Your doubles told me you had both the missing kings. And I could have made the contract just as well without finessing in hearts. If I had played to the heart ace and run the clubs, you would have been squeezed in three suits instead of two, and you would have had to give me two tricks however you discarded."

April 4, 1970

A DOUBLE CONFUSION LEADS TO A SWING OF 4,790 POINTS

Two unusual confusions, one on each side, prepared the way for a lead decision that swung almost 5,000 points on the diagramed deal.

It was played in a Westchester Winners Game at the Rye Community Synagogue, and was reported by Frank Adams of Rye, New York, a member of *The New York Times* editorial board. He held the North hand, and had no suspicion of the dramatic developments that were to follow his opening bid of one diamond.

East's jump to four hearts crowded the auction for South, James Aberle of Old Greenwich, Connecticut, who made the ambiguous bid of four notrump. He intended this to be "unusual," indicating length in the unbid black suits, but was aware that his partner might interpret it as Blackwood, as many would.

North was also aware of the ambiguity, but diagnosed his partner's intentions correctly and bid five spades.

As it was, South decided, rather arbitrarily, that his partner has shown three aces rather than a genuine spade suit. So when his opponents bid seven hearts he took a wild gamble by bidding seven notrump instead of the obvious bid of seven spades.

However, it was East–West's turn to be confused when East doubled seven notrump. A double of a slam by the player not on lead is normally a Lightner double, asking for an unusual lead that will frequently be in a suit bid by dummy.

West interpreted the double in this sense, and after protracted thought led the diamond queen. It was just possible from his angle that his partner held the diamond ace instead of the heart ace, in which the declarer could perhaps make the heart ace and twelve black-suit tricks after a heart lead.

East was naturally upset when his partner led a diamond, giving the declarer 2,490 instead of 2,300 to the defense. East argued that he would not have sacrificed to seven hearts if he had held a sure defensive trick against seven clubs. North and South did not argue at all—they just counted their blessings.

JULY 27, 1967

NORTH (D)
♠ A K 7 3
♡ 8
♢ A K 10 6
♣ J 9 4 3

WEST
♠ 8 4
♡ Q 10 7 2
♢ Q J 9 8 3
♣ 6 2

EAST
♠ J 6
♡ A K J 9 6 5 4 3
♢ 5 4
♣ 7

SOUTH
♠ Q 10 9 5 2
♡ —
♢ 7 2
♣ A K Q 10 8 5

Both sides were vulnerable.
The bidding:

NORTH	EAST	SOUTH	WEST
1 ♢	4 ♡	4 NT	5 ♡
5 ♠	6 ♡	7 ♣	7 ♡
Dbl.	Pass	7 NT	Pass
Pass	Dbl.	Pass	Pass
Pass			

West led the diamond queen.

MEMORIES OF A GREAT TOURNAMENT DIRECTOR

Al Sobel of New York City, perhaps the world's most celebrated tournament director, retired in 1968 from his position as tournament manager of the American Contract Bridge League. Players all over North America missed the stentorian tones that controlled more than a thousand tournaments in thirty-five years. To make sure of the attention of his audience, Sobel invariably barked an ambiguous "You!" into his microphone in a voice that any sergeant major would envy—and five hundred players guiltily abandoned their conversations to pay attention to the official announcements.

For many years Sobel wrote an entertaining monthly column entitled "Thirty Days" in the *American Contract Bridge League Bulletin*. In it he described his wanderings in various parts of the world, including South America, the Far East, and Russia, and supplied his readers with a wealth of bridge anecdotage. At one time he incautiously introduced the subject of bridge "Swifties" and was deluged by adverbial puns. He contributed one of the best himself: "I should have bid a slam," he said morbidly.

Sobel seldom reported bridge hands, but a few years ago his column included one of the saddest and funniest stories in the history of the game:

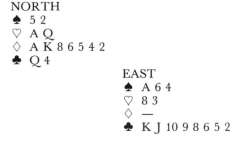

```
            NORTH
            ♠ 5 2
            ♡ A Q
            ◇ A K 8 6 5 4 2
            ♣ Q 4
                          EAST
                          ♠ A 6 4
                          ♡ 8 3
                          ◇ —
                          ♣ K J 10 9 8 6 5 2
```

You sit East defending six spades doubled after the auction shown in the diagram.

Your Lightner double of six spades asked for an unusual lead,

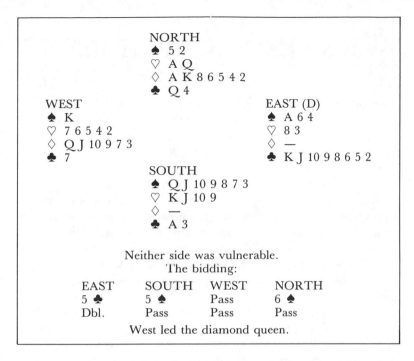

NORTH
♠ 5 2
♡ A Q
♢ A K 8 6 5 4 2
♣ Q 4

WEST
♠ K
♡ 7 6 5 4 2
♢ Q J 10 9 7 3
♣ 7

EAST (D)
♠ A 6 4
♡ 8 3
♢ —
♣ K J 10 9 8 6 5 2

SOUTH
♠ Q J 10 9 8 7 3
♡ K J 10 9
♢ —
♣ A 3

Neither side was vulnerable.
The bidding:

EAST	SOUTH	WEST	NORTH
5 ♣	5 ♠	Pass	6 ♠
Dbl.	Pass	Pass	Pass

West led the diamond queen.

and your partner obligingly led the diamond queen rather than a club. You ruff dummy's king happily, but are less happy when declarer overruffs.

Worse is to come. South leads the heart nine to dummy's ace, and plays the diamond ace. Determined to prevent a club discard, you ruff low and the whole deal turns out to be as shown.

South overruffs again, leads a heart to dummy's queen, and plays a trump. You win with the spade ace, on which your partner drops the king with a hurt look. To add insult to injury you are now endplayed. Whatever club you choose to lead, the declarer makes the queen and the ace, making his doubled slam.

This deal was really played in a game in Canada, and the unknown South brought off a remarkable swindle.

East was so disgusted that he quit the game.

April 21, 1968

WRONG REASON, RIGHT RESULT

One of the best collections of deals ever published is *More Tales of Hoffman*, by Martin Hoffman of London. The author circulates widely on the international circuit, and many of the themes he presents are highly original. On the diagramed deal the opening lead proved to be devastating.

East opened four spades, and eventually ventured a greedy double of six hearts. This was a match-point event, and he was trying for an extra 50 points. He should have reasoned that he would have a good score in any event if the slam failed.

West was Louis Tarlo of London, a veteran who has represented Britain on many occasions both as player and captain. After some thought he produced a devastating lead: the diamond king.

This proved to be a blind Merrimac Coup, removing a vital entry from the dummy. With any other lead South would have had no trouble in drawing trumps and establishing clubs, but now the contract was in trouble.

South should no doubt have played a club immediately after taking the diamond ace, for it would not have been easy for East to make the essential ducking play. Instead, however, South played for a quick diamond ruff, and East overruffed to defeat the slam.

Everyone was ready to lavish praise on Tarlo for the brilliance of his lead, but he felt obliged to confess the truth. He had assumed that his partner was making a Lightner double, asking for an unusual lead. East was presumably void in one of the minor suits.

The purpose of the diamond king was to retain the lead in the West hand if East happened to hold the diamond ace and a club void. If East held a diamond void and the club ace, then any diamond lead would serve.

A brilliant lead indeed, but for quite the wrong reason.

SEPTEMBER 4, 1968

NORTH
♠ 6 5 3
♡ 6 3
◇ A 4
♣ K Q J 10 8 7

WEST
♠ 9 2
♡ J 4 2
◇ K 10 9 6 5
♣ 6 5 3

EAST (D)
♠ K Q J 10 8 7 4
♡ 8 5
◇ 7 2
♣ A 9

SOUTH
♠ A
♡ A K Q 10 9 7
◇ Q J 8 3
♣ 4 2

Neither side was vulnerable.
The bidding:

EAST	SOUTH	WEST	NORTH
4 ♠	Dbl.	Pass	6 ♣
Pass	6 ♡	Pass	Pass
Dbl.	Pass	Pass	Pass

West led the diamond king.

No Double, Lead Trouble

Aiming to become, at sixty-nine, the oldest American ever to compete in a Bermuda Bowl world championship contest, veteran star B. Jay Becker qualified for national play-offs.

The first match opened sensationally. On the very first deal both teams reached an excellent grand slam that was not easy to bid. Thirteen tricks were guaranteed in either major suit unless the defenders could achieve a ruff in the other major.

In such circumstances a five-five fit is distinctly safer than a five-four fit, because a 3-0 break in the side suit is about twice as likely as a 4-0 break. But it was not so on this occasion, and the opposing team was entitled to feel that the fates were not on its side. South opened with one heart, and showed a powerful hand by raising the one spade response to game. North used Blackwood, locating two aces and one king in his partner's hand. He then had the information he needed to bid the grand slam, and he bid it in hearts rather than spades for two very good reasons.

First, the danger of a heart ruff exceeded the danger of a spade ruff, for the partnership clearly held more hearts than spades.

Second, and more important, South's distribution might be 4-5-2-2, in which case the spade suit would provide a discard for a diamond loser playing in seven hearts, but there would be no discard in spades.

A significant but unobstrusive feature of the auction was East's pass over seven hearts. The East player was Becker, who was of course aware that he could double seven hearts to ask West to lead a spade. But he also realized that the double would alert his opponents to the situation, and they would seize the opportunity to shift into seven spades, against which there was unlikely to be any defense.

So Becker passed, without any revealing hesitation that could have created an ethical problem, hoping that his partner would lead a spade in spite of the absence of a Lightner double to ask for a spade lead.

Jeff Rubens as West took a long time over the opening lead, but finally made the winning decision and led a spade to defeat the grand slam. He knew from the bidding that North–South held at least four spades each. If they held exactly four the lead

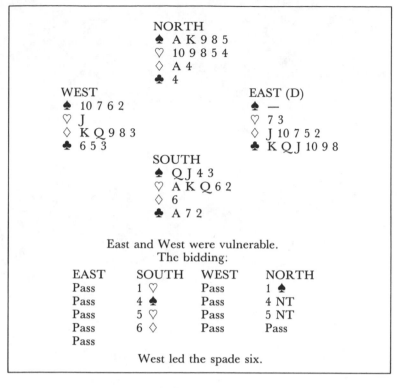

NORTH
♠ A K 9 8 5
♡ 10 9 8 5 4
♢ A 4
♣ 4

WEST
♠ 10 7 6 2
♡ J
♢ K Q 9 8 3
♣ 6 5 3

EAST (D)
♠ —
♡ 7 3
♢ J 10 7 5 2
♣ K Q J 10 9 8

SOUTH
♠ Q J 4 3
♡ A K Q 6 2
♢ 6
♣ A 7 2

East and West were vulnerable.
The bidding:

EAST	SOUTH	WEST	NORTH
Pass	1 ♡	Pass	1 ♠
Pass	4 ♠	Pass	4 NT
Pass	5 ♡	Pass	5 NT
Pass	6 ♢	Pass	Pass
Pass			

West led the spade six.

would do no harm, because there would be no discard to come. And he could not afford to give up the chance that his partner would be able to ruff.

In the replay East crowded the auction with an opening bid of three clubs. South made a takeout double, and both players proceeded to cue-bid in clubs to show slam ambitions.

North then made an imaginative jump to seven spades, choosing the stronger suit. He wanted to be the declarer for the good reason that on the bidding East was more likely than West to have a void suit and be able to ruff the opening lead.

And so it proved. Seven spades made easily, and the Becker team gained 17 international match points.

OCTOBER 2, 1972

3

THE PLAY'S
THE THING

Here we have a quintet of brilliant performances by declarers in doubled contracts, the first two by New York experts. One offers an unexpected trick, the other concedes an unexpected trick, and both West players wind up feeling foolish. Then a double helps a Californian star to make a slam that appears hopeless, we take a ride off into the Wild West, and a German expert uncovers an exotic ending.

Making Tricks Without Straw

In rubber bridge the player has no difficulty in determining his primary target. He is trying to make his contract, or to defeat an opposing contract if he is a defender. If this primary target is either simple or impossible to achieve, his attention is inclined to wander.

In duplicate, player has much more trouble in identifying his target. An overtrick may be more important than making the contract, and the precise number of tricks by which his contract is defeated may make the difference between a top or a bottom score.

It was this consideration that impelled Manuel Goodman of Manhattan Beach to make a daring play in the diagramed deal. As South, he had considerable reserve strength for his overcall of one spade and persevered to four spades when East–West reached their heart game. There seemed a good chance of making eight tricks in four spades doubled, which would be an economical save.

The declarer did not feel very happy when West led the jack of hearts against four spades doubled and the dummy appeared. East had doubled with the confident air of a man holding three good trumps, and there was a real danger in the absence of entries to dummy of losing six tricks. A penalty of 500 would be a disaster for North–South, because at other tables East would presumably score 420 or 450 in four hearts.

Goodman, therefore, made an imaginative and unusual play after ruffing the first trick. Giving up the slight chance that the club queen would fall in two rounds, he led the club ten.

West looked at the club ten suspiciously, and then played low. Surely South would not underlead the ace–king of clubs? But South had. He overtook the club ten with dummy's jack, and his primary objective of making eight tricks was now within reach.

It was time to lead trumps, and he carefully led the spade six in preference to the nine. East played the five, unwisely assuming that his partner could beat the six, and was disappointed. Dummy retained the lead, and the spade nine was led.

East rose belatedly with his ace, and hoped for a minor-suit ruff. He should no doubt have led the diamond ace, to see if his

```
                    NORTH
                    ♠ 9 6
                    ♡ Q 3 2
                    ◊ J 8 5 3
                    ♣ J 7 6 5
WEST                                    EAST (D)
♠ 2                                     ♠ A Q 5
♡ J 10 6 5                              ♡ A K 9 8 7 4
◊ K 10 9 2                              ◊ A 4
♣ Q 8 3 2                               ♣ 9 4
                    SOUTH
                    ♠ K J 10 8 7 4 3
                    ♡ —
                    ◊ Q 7 6
                    ♣ A K 10
```

Neither side was vulnerable.
The bidding:

EAST	SOUTH	WEST	NORTH
1 ♡	1 ♠	2 ♡	Pass
4 ♡	4 ♠	Pass	Pass
Dbl.	Pass	Pass	Pass

West led the heart jack.

partner would produce an encouraging signal. But he was as deceived as his partner had been by South's club play. He led a club, expecting West to have the ace, and South now made his contract.

He won the club shift, cashed the spade king to draw East's queen, and led the diamond queen. As East was marked with three spades and heart length, there was a fair chance that he held a doubleton diamond honor. A low diamond lead—hoping for West to have a doubleton diamond honor—was far less likely to succeed.

West won with the diamond king and led another heart. South ruffed and ducked a diamond. This gave him ten tricks—and his contract—when other declarers were making seven.

MARCH 1, 1966

ANOTHER GOREN MOVING UP; HE'S NOT RELATED TO CHARLES

If every bridge player in the United States were polled and asked to name a famous player, the most popular choice would probably be Charles Goren, a dominant figure in the 1940s and 1950s and the author of many successful books on the game. He retired from active tournament play nearly two decades ago, and is a shadowy historical figure to the younger generation of players.

However, the Goren name may be due for a revival. The 1980 New England Regional Knockout Championship in Hartford was won by a group that included Barry Goren of New York—no relation to Charles. At nineteen he is probably the youngest player ever to win this prestigious fifty-year-old title. A babe in arms when Charles Goren last played competitively, he may be headed for equal fame.

Like most young experts, Goren is an aggressive and optimistic bidder. On the diagramed deal, played at the Beverly East Club in New York City, he opened the South hand with two clubs, strong and artificial. The graybeards would be more likely to bid one heart or four hearts.

The bidding got out of hand, as far as South was concerned, when West jumped pre-emptively to five clubs and North bid five spades. It is worth considering how that contract would have fared, but South was not willing to put the matter to the test. He bid six hearts, and East was happy to double.

The club king was led, and when the dummy appeared, Goren regretted his decision to bid over five spades. There seemed no chance to make twelve tricks.

Feeling that he might as well be hung for a sheep as for a lamb, Goren tried a little gambit by ducking the opening lead. This puzzled West, who tried to think of some reason for South to duck. He did not find one, however, and continued passively with another club.

This gave Goren the opportunity he wanted. He threw his spade king on the club ace and cashed the heart ten. He then ruffed out the spade ace and made all the remaining tricks. There was still a trump entry to the dummy, and the diamonds in the

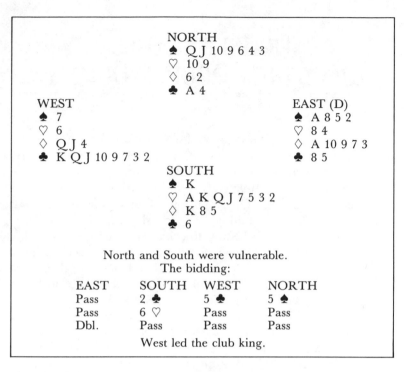

NORTH
♠ Q J 10 9 6 4 3
♡ 10 9
◇ 6 2
♣ A 4

WEST
♠ 7
♡ 6
◇ Q J 4
♣ K Q J 10 9 7 3 2

EAST (D)
♠ A 8 5 2
♡ 8 4
◇ A 10 9 7 3
♣ 8 5

SOUTH
♠ K
♡ A K Q J 7 5 3 2
◇ K 8 5
♣ 6

North and South were vulnerable.
The bidding:

EAST	SOUTH	WEST	NORTH
Pass	2 ♣	5 ♣	5 ♠
Pass	6 ♡	Pass	Pass
Dbl.	Pass	Pass	Pass

West led the club king.

closed hand were discarded on spades. East was not happy, and spoke strongly to his partner in the postmortem.

Note that North would probably have made five spades. To defeat it East would have to lead a heart rather than his partner's club suit or one of his aces, and he would be unlikely to think of that.

July 14, 1980

DOUBLE MAKES
DECLARER DOUBLE-DUMMY

Most of the swings in head-to-head matches result from decisions in the bidding in which judgment and luck both play a part. Some swings result from the choice of opening lead or from the quality of the defense. Relatively few are attributable to the quality of the dummy play: On 90 percent of deals, the declarer will adopt similar strategies and will achieve similar results.

Few experts can be relied on to consistently find the best play on those rare hands in which the dummy play presents a high degree of difficulty. Among that select band is Eddie Kantar of Los Angeles, whose brilliant effort on the diagrammed deal was reported by a Californian writer, Mike Shuman.

The bidding was spectacular. West's jump to two diamonds over one club was pre-emptive, and North showed club support. East emerged with an unexpected cue-bid in clubs, which West correctly interpreted to mean great length in the major suits.

It was South's turn to make a cue-bid, in diamonds, and West ventured four spades on his three-card suit. When North bid five clubs, South continued to six, not so much because he expected to make it as because he expected his opponents to sacrifice. They didn't.

West led the diamond king, and Kantar, as South, studied the position for five minutes in the hope of finding a road to twelve tricks. One possibility was to ruff diamonds repeatedly in the South hand and hope to develop a squeeze. But for a squeeze to work, a trick must be given up, presumably in hearts, and the defenders can continue hearts to remove a vital entry from the South hand.

The final double was a useful clue to the position of the high cards, and Kantar came up with a winning play, which is hard to see with all the cards in view.

He ruffed the opening lead, drew trumps ending in dummy, and led the spade jack. He would have played low if East had refused to cover, but East put on the queen and the ace won.

A spade was ruffed in dummy, and the closed hand was re-entered with a diamond ruff. The spade ten was led, successfully

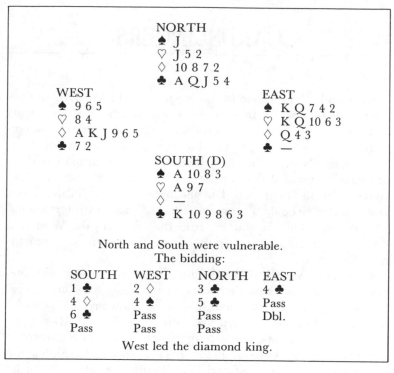

NORTH
♠ J
♡ J 5 2
◇ 10 8 7 2
♣ A Q J 5 4

WEST
♠ 9 6 5
♡ 8 4
◇ A K J 9 6 5
♣ 7 2

EAST
♠ K Q 7 4 2
♡ K Q 10 6 3
◇ Q 4 3
♣ —

SOUTH (D)
♠ A 10 8 3
♡ A 9 7
◇ —
♣ K 10 9 8 6 3

North and South were vulnerable.
The bidding:

SOUTH	WEST	NORTH	EAST
1 ♣	2 ◇	3 ♣	4 ♣
4 ◇	4 ♠	5 ♣	Pass
6 ♣	Pass	Pass	Dbl.
Pass	Pass	Pass	

West led the diamond king.

pinning West's crucial ninespot, and a heart was discarded from dummy, a loser-on-loser play.

East won with the spade king, and South claimed the slam. His spade eight was now a winner, providing a discard for the remaining heart loser in the dummy.

South received well-deserved congratulations, and West was wrapped in gloom. "I should have led a heart," he announced sadly.

SEPTEMBER 21, 1971

CARDSLINGERS

Heroes and villains shooting at each other in Western movies often find themselves in a tricky situation where action seems called for but any move will create a target and lead to disaster.

Bridge players may also be in a position in which any move is fatal, especially when they find themselves in the rugged Far West as in the diagramed deal in the 1974 Spring Nationals in Vancouver, British Columbia. The sharpshooting hero in the South seat was Dr. Ronald Forbes, a former Canadian international who now lives in Vancouver. And the villain in the West seat was a gunslinging expert from out of town who shall remain nameless.

Our hero opened the South hand in the fourth seat with one heart. And when his partner responded one notrump and he rebid two hearts, it seemed that the auction had come to a peaceful conclusion. But East opened fire with a double, and when West passed everyone knew it was a fight to the death. If South could make eight tricks he would gallop to a top score with 670, leaving the lifeless bodies of East and West beside the table. But if he failed he would lose at least 200 points, losing to all part-scores made in the opposite direction.

A glance at the diagram suggests that South, like all Western heroes, was facing hopeless odds. He was outnumbered two-to-one and might be expected to lose seven tricks, four in trumps and one in each side suit.

West opened the main battle by shooting out the club queen. When this held the trick he continued the suit, and South evened the score by ruffing. He led a diamond, and West hopped up with the ace. This was the right play, since he did not want to be given the lead later in diamonds and be short of exit cards.

West played back a diamond, and South won in the dummy. If South had been able to peek, he would have ruffed a club at this point and led the heart king with good effect. But both villains were holding their cards close to their chests.

So South led a heart and put his king on East's queen. West, somewhat shortsighted like all villains, snatched the trick with the heart ace and settled down to think—too late. He should have ducked. The position was now this:

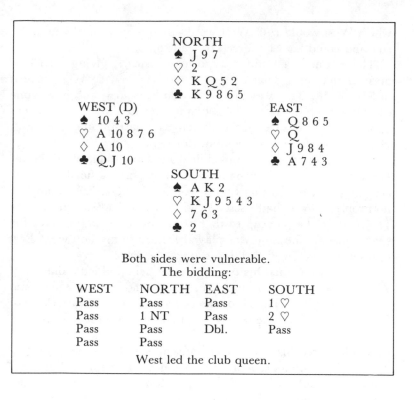

NORTH
♠ J 9 7
♡ 2
◇ K Q 5 2
♣ K 9 8 6 5

WEST (D)
♠ 10 4 3
♡ A 10 8 7 6
◇ A 10
♣ Q J 10

EAST
♠ Q 8 6 5
♡ Q
◇ J 9 8 4
♣ A 7 4 3

SOUTH
♠ A K 2
♡ K J 9 5 4 3
◇ 7 6 3
♣ 2

Both sides were vulnerable.
The bidding:

WEST	NORTH	EAST	SOUTH
Pass	Pass	Pass	1 ♡
Pass	1 NT	Pass	2 ♡
Pass	Pass	Dbl.	Pass
Pass	Pass		

West led the club queen.

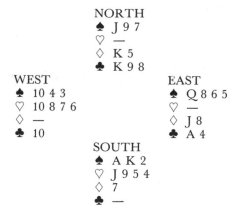

NORTH
♠ J 9 7
♡ —
◇ K 5
♣ K 9 8

WEST
♠ 10 4 3
♡ 10 8 7 6
◇ —
♣ 10

EAST
♠ Q 8 6 5
♡ —
◇ J 8
♣ A 4

SOUTH
♠ A K 2
♡ J 9 5 4
◇ 7
♣ —

The obvious lead at this point for the villainous West was a club, since a heart lead or a spade lead is immediately helpful to the declarer. West would then have been endplayed twice for a two-trick gain for South. He would ruff and lead a diamond, which West would ruff. West would then have to lead one major suit and could later be forced to lead the other.

The second possibility was to lead a heart, giving a trick at once in that suit. That seemed a foolish play, so West gave it little thought. This was lucky for South, who would have gone down after a heart return. West continues to play hearts at every opportunity and saves his club ten as a last-minute exit card, giving the declarer one trick but not two.

West settled for a third possibility and led a spade at this point. He knew that South probably held three spades headed by the ace–king, but hoped that South would misguess. But South had no problem. West had passed originally and had shown up with 11 points in the play up to that point. So East had to have the spade queen. The nine was played from dummy and won. East refused to cover, which did not affect the issue.

Next South cashed his two spade winners and led a diamond. West ruffed and led a club. But South had the last laugh and virtue triumphed. The club was ruffed and a low heart was led, forcing a lead from the ten–eight of trumps into the jack–nine at the finish.

South scored his 670 points and galloped off, leaving two severely injured opponents. East took out his own gun and pumped a few more bullets into West. "We don't need villains around here," he opined, "who don't know how to handle their trumps in a shootout."

APRIL 28, 1974

THE SCHROEDER SQUEEZE

A curious resemblance can be found between the scientists who specialize in electronics and the bridge scientists who specialize in squeezes. Both groups deal in miracles that the general public admires without comprehension, and both groups try to perform their miracles in smaller and smaller spaces.

Most textbooks imply that the esoteric squeezes need at least a four-card ending, but they are wrong. Here, for example is a three-card triple squeeze:

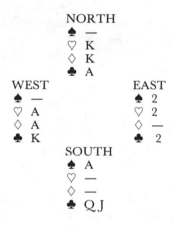

NORTH
♠ —
♡ K
◇ K
♣ A

WEST
♠ —
♡ A
◇ A
♣ K

EAST
♠ 2
♡ 2
◇ —
♣ 2

SOUTH
♠ A
♡ —
◇ —
♣ Q J

The contract is notrump, and South has the lead. He has only two sure tricks, but the lead of the spade ace pinches West in three suits. If he throws one of his aces, South discards the other red suit and makes the last two tricks in the dummy. And if he discards the club king, South discards the club ace and makes two winners in his hand.

A triple squeeze in a three-card position can even be managed "without the count," that is, in a position in which the defense takes a trick after the squeeze.

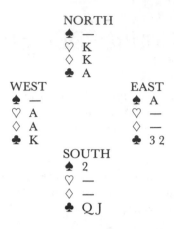

NORTH
♠ —
♡ K
◇ K
♣ A

WEST
♠ —
♡ A
◇ A
♣ K

EAST
♠ A
♡ —
◇ —
♣ 3 2

SOUTH
♠ 2
♡ —
◇ —
♣ Q J

This is rather like the previous diagram. The North and West hands are identical, but South has a spade loser instead of a winner. He leads the spade loser, and West is in trouble again. If he discards an ace, South will end up with two winners in dummy, and if he discards his king, South unblocks the club ace and makes the last two tricks in his hand. For a little extra spice one could give South the queen–ten of clubs and East the guarded jack.

The ultimate in three-card squeeze endings occurred in West Germany on the diagramed deal. One of Europe's leading player-writers, Dirk Schroeder of Wiesbaden, found himself the happy beneficiary of a "triple trump squeeze without the count." As before, a trick had to be lost to the defense after one defender had been squeezed in three suits, but this time there was a vital ruffing element.

In a pair contest Schroeder as South made a flimsy overcall of one spade over one club. His partner competed as far as three spades, and East showed extra strength with a double that West passed for penalties. Clubs were led and continued, and South ruffed. He led a low spade and might have finessed the nine when West played low. However, he played the ace from dummy and finessed the heart ten successfully.

The next move was to surrender a diamond trick, and East won and played a third round of clubs. South ruffed, ruffed a diamond, and finessed the heart queen. Now the heart ace was led, and West ruffed and played a diamond. This was ruffed in dummy with the spade nine, and the position was:

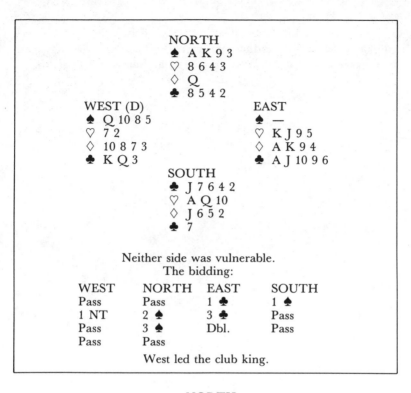

```
                    NORTH
                    ♠ A K 9 3
                    ♡ 8 6 4 3
                    ◇ Q
                    ♣ 8 5 4 2
    WEST (D)                        EAST
    ♠ Q 10 8 5                      ♠ —
    ♡ 7 2                           ♡ K J 9 5
    ◇ 10 8 7 3                      ◇ A K 9 4
    ♣ K Q 3                         ♣ A J 10 9 6
                    SOUTH
                    ♣ J 7 6 4 2
                    ♡ A Q 10
                    ◇ J 6 5 2
                    ♣ 7
```

Neither side was vulnerable.
The bidding:

WEST	NORTH	EAST	SOUTH
Pass	Pass	1 ♣	1 ♠
1 NT	2 ♠	3 ♣	Pass
Pass	3 ♠	Dbl.	Pass
Pass	Pass		

West led the club king.

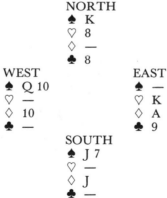

```
                NORTH
                ♠ K
                ♡ 8
                ◇ —
                ♣ 8
    WEST                    EAST
    ♠ Q 10                  ♠ —
    ♡ —                     ♡ K
    ◇ 10                    ◇ A
    ♣ —                     ♣ 9
                SOUTH
                ♠ J 7
                ♡ —
                ◇ J
                ♣ —
```

The spade king was led from dummy, and East had to part
with one of his winners. If he threw a heart or a club, he would
have established a winner in dummy which South would have
led at the next trick. So East threw the diamond ace.

Now South led from the dummy and ruffed. West had to over-ruff, and South's diamond jack won the last trick. Bridge text-books of the future will have to call it the Schroeder squeeze.

July 14, 1974

DYNAMITE DEFENSE

The first two deals feature the American player Lou Bluhm, first in a minor supporting role and then in a major one. Then there is a brilliancy by America's top-ranked player and a weird series of defensive plays. The last deal allows the reader to test himself on a very difficult hand from France.

THINK BEFORE YOU PITCH

Total beginners from the days of whist have been taught that they should never trump their partner's trick. But experts know better, and Tom Sanders of Nashville, the nonplaying captain of the 1981 United States world championship team, gave a good demonstration of this unusual play on the diagramed deal, from the 1981 life master pairs qualifying.

At almost all tables East–West played in four hearts, a contract that often failed because the declarer did not solve the problems created by the bad trump break. Sanders and his partner, Lou Bluhm of Atlanta, were headed in the same direction, but another possibility opened up for them.

East's jump to two notrump in response to the one-heart opening was "Jacoby," showing a good hand with a heart fit. When South ventured to bid his clubs at the three-level, Bluhm doubled, hoping to collect 500 points instead of a nonvulnerable game. Sanders, as East, accepted this suggestion, and his partner led the heart ace.

This was not a great success, for South ruffed and led the diamond ace. Another diamond lead was taken by the king, and East shifted to the spade nine. West took the jack and the king, leading to this distribution:

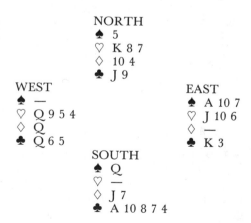

```
                    NORTH
                    ♠ 5
                    ♡ K 8 7
                    ◇ 10 4
                    ♣ J 9
      WEST                        EAST
      ♠ —                         ♠ A 10 7
      ♡ Q 9 5 4                   ♡ J 10 6
      ◇ Q                         ◇ —
      ♣ Q 6 5                     ♣ K 3
                    SOUTH
                    ♠ Q
                    ♡ —
                    ◇ J 7
                    ♣ A 10 8 7 4
```

When Bluhm led the diamond queen, an obvious winner,

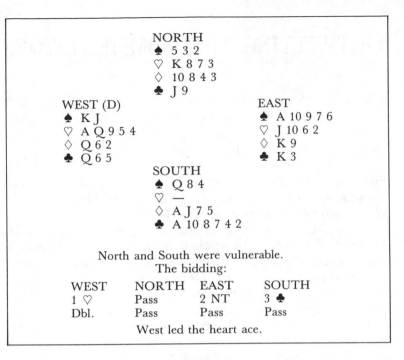

NORTH
♠ 5 3 2
♡ K 8 7 3
◊ 10 8 4 3
♣ J 9

WEST (D)
♠ K J
♡ A Q 9 5 4
◊ Q 6 2
♣ Q 6 5

EAST
♠ A 10 9 7 6
♡ J 10 6 2
◊ K 9
♣ K 3

SOUTH
♠ Q 8 4
♡ —
◊ A J 7 5
♣ A 10 8 7 4 2

North and South were vulnerable.
The bidding:

WEST	NORTH	EAST	SOUTH
1 ♡	Pass	2 NT	3 ♣
Dbl.	Pass	Pass	Pass

West led the heart ace.

Sanders thought it over and ruffed. He cashed his spade ace, and the defense later made a trump for down two. East–West had achieved their target of a two-trick defeat and had earned all the match points.

Notice that if East had discarded on the diamond lead, the spade ace would have withered on the vine. Sooner or later, South would have thrown the spade queen on dummy's heart king. The best West could do would be to shift to a trump, and when the trumps had disappeared, the diamond ten would serve as an entry to dummy. South would have unblocked his diamond jack on the third round of the suit.

JULY 28, 1981

OUTWITTING THE COMMENTATORS

If there had been a prize for the best defensive play of 1974, Steve Goldberg of Marietta, Georgia, would have been a strong candidate for his effort on the diagramed deal, played in the International Team Trials in Washington.

Goldberg as West opened one diamond, and it was well for him that South did not venture to make a penalty pass when North made a takeout double. One diamond doubled would have gone down two or three tricks, for 500 or 800.

South did not think his diamonds were strong enough to pass. His one notrump bid showed moderate strength and a stopper in diamonds, so North raised to game. A black-suit lead would have been best for the defense, but Goldberg naturally led diamonds. Like many other experts he does not subscribe to the traditional fourth-best leads, and his choice was the deuce.

He was not particularly happy when South won with the seven, but the declarer had his own worries. With the lead in his hand he took the opportunity to finesse the heart ten, but East produced the jack. A spade was returned to the king and ace, and South continued by playing a heart to the king. West won with the ace and had to lead in this crucial position:

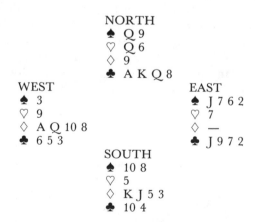

```
                    NORTH
                    ♠ Q 9
                    ♡ Q 6
                    ◇ 9
                    ♣ A K Q 8
     WEST                          EAST
     ♠ 3                           ♠ J 7 6 2
     ♡ 9                           ♡ 7
     ◇ A Q 10 8                    ◇ —
     ♣ 6 5 3                       ♣ J 9 7 2
                    SOUTH
                    ♠ 10 8
                    ♡ 5
                    ◇ K J 5 3
                    ♣ 10 4
```

The commentators watching the play on Vugraph, and seeing all four hands, expected Goldberg to return a spade. They worked

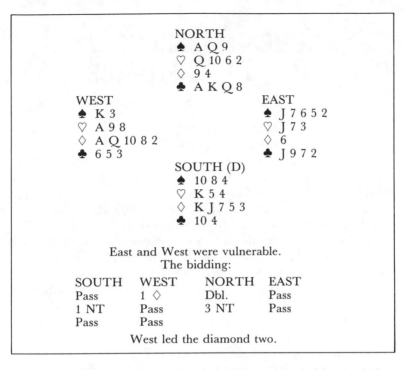

NORTH
♠ A Q 9
♡ Q 10 6 2
◇ 9 4
♣ A K Q 8

WEST
♠ K 3
♡ A 9 8
◇ A Q 10 8 2
♣ 6 5 3

EAST
♠ J 7 6 5 2
♡ J 7 3
◇ 6
♣ J 9 7 2

SOUTH (D)
♠ 10 8 4
♡ K 5 4
◇ K J 7 5 3
♣ 10 4

East and West were vulnerable.
The bidding:

SOUTH	WEST	NORTH	EAST
Pass	1 ◇	Dbl.	Pass
1 NT	Pass	3 NT	Pass
Pass	Pass		

West led the diamond two.

out that the contract could then be made and probably would be. South would take all dummy's winners and finally lead a diamond. West would have nothing but diamonds and be forced to give South his ninth trick in that suit.

There was an unusual way to frustrate that line of play, and Goldberg found it. He cashed the diamond ace, deliberately establishing South's king, before exiting with a spade. By so doing he removed the diamond in dummy, which was necessary to operate the throw-in.

South did the best he could. He took the spade queen and the two heart winners, forcing East down to the spade jack and four clubs. A spade led from dummy now threw the lead to East, but a defensive counter was available.

A low club return would have given South the last four tricks, but Goldberg's partner, Lou Bluhm of Atlanta, Georgia, rose to the occasion by returning the club jack. This left the suit blocked, and South had to choose between conceding the last trick to East in clubs or to West in diamonds.

SEPTEMBER 13, 1974

CHEAP OVERRUFFS
CAN BE EXPENSIVE

One of the most exciting matches ever played on a major American occasion took place in Memphis in 1985. After wild oscillations in the score and a nail-biting finish, it determined the composition of the United States team in that year's world championship in São Paulo, Brazil.

In the diagramed deal from the match, Bob Hamman of Dallas demonstrated his superb defensive skill. He held the East cards, and wound up defending five diamonds doubled after a wildly competitive auction. He and Bob Wolff, also of Dallas, had reached four spades, which would have made without difficulty since the bidding suggested that North was likely to have spade length.

But Marty Bergen of White Plains, New York, as South, was naturally reluctant to defend with five–seven in the minor suits. In the light of the previous bidding, his four notrump bid asked his partner to choose a minor, with a preference for clubs. Five clubs doubled would obviously have failed by two tricks, but North chose five diamonds, also doubled, and that proved to be tricky. The question was whether South could establish and use his clubs without losing control.

A spade was led, and Hamman did not make the mistake of playing the ace when dummy played low. His jack was ruffed by the declarer, who cashed the club ace and ruffed a club with dummy's eight. Nine hundred ninety-nine players out of a thousand would overruff and find that they had defeated the contract by one trick.

South would ruff the next spade lead, ruff another club with the diamond jack, and draw trumps. When the remaining trumps divided conveniently, he would heave a sigh of relief and surrender a club trick. The clubs would be established with the last trump as an entry, and the defense would have three tricks and a score of 200.

But Hamman saw this coming, and instead of the obvious overruff he brilliantly discarded a heart. Now there was no way for Bergen to establish and use his clubs. He led a heart from

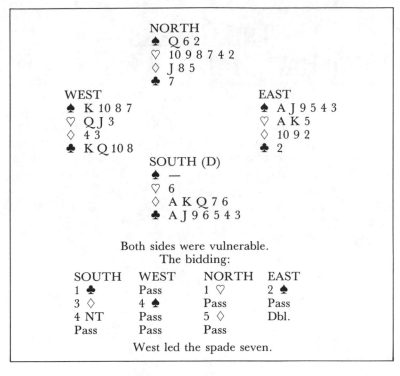

NORTH
♠ Q 6 2
♡ 10 9 8 7 4 2
◊ J 8 5
♣ 7

WEST
♠ K 10 8 7
♡ Q J 3
◊ 4 3
♣ K Q 10 8

EAST
♠ A J 9 5 4 3
♡ A K 5
◊ 10 9 2
♣ 2

SOUTH (D)
♠ —
♡ 6
◊ A K Q 7 6
♣ A J 9 6 5 4 3

Both sides were vulnerable.
The bidding:

SOUTH	WEST	NORTH	EAST
1 ♣	Pass	1 ♡	2 ♠
3 ◊	4 ♠	Pass	Pass
4 NT	Pass	5 ◊	Dbl.
Pass	Pass	Pass	

West led the spade seven.

dummy and was forced to ruff a second spade lead. He ruffed a
club with the diamond jack, scoring the remaining trumps in his
hand, but that was just eight tricks and a penalty of 800.

In the replay the same contract was reached, failing by two
tricks after a trump lead for a penalty of 500. If Hamman had
routinely overruffed, his team would have lost 7 points instead of
gaining them, and would eventually have lost the match instead
of winning it.

June 2, 1985

THE GREEKS
MUST HAVE HAD A WORD FOR IT

In most of the world, and at most of the world's bridge tables, shortages are a recurring problem. But in rare circumstances the problem may be one of oversupply. In Western Europe it relates to butter. And in the diagramed deal, played in Greece, it concerned trumps.

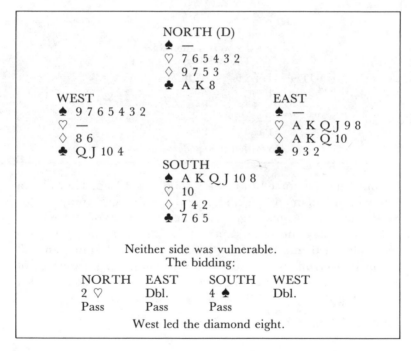

NORTH (D)
♠ —
♡ 7 6 5 4 3 2
◇ 9 7 5 3
♣ A K 8

WEST
♠ 9 7 6 5 4 3 2
♡ —
◇ 8 6
♣ Q J 10 4

EAST
♠ —
♡ A K Q J 9 8
◇ A K Q 10
♣ 9 3 2

SOUTH
♠ A K Q J 10 8
♡ 10
◇ J 4 2
♣ 7 6 5

Neither side was vulnerable.
The bidding:

NORTH	EAST	SOUTH	WEST
2 ♡	Dbl.	4 ♠	Dbl.
Pass	Pass	Pass	

West led the diamond eight.

The setting was a duplicate game at the American Club in Athens. At many tables East played in four hearts, which could not be defeated. At others South did better by playing four spades doubled and escaping for down two.

But at one table the South cards were held by Warren Dix, and he ruefully reported some brilliant defense by the West player, Greta Germanos. Dix played in four spades doubled after his partner had disconcerted East with a somewhat eccentric weak two-bid.

The opening lead was the diamond eight, and when East won with the queen, he shifted to the heart ace. He got his second shock when his partner, correctly foreseeing an excess of trumps, ruffed the heart winner and led her remaining diamond.

East won and led another diamond winner, on which West discarded the club queen. East reverted to hearts, and when Dix ruffed with the spade ace, West underruffed.

"By this time," reports Dix, "all of us were confused by Greta's weird series of plays." He led the spade king, and the position became clear when East discarded a heart. The position was now this:

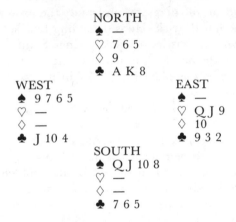

NORTH
♠ —
♡ 7 6 5
◇ 9
♣ A K 8

WEST
♠ 9 7 6 5
♡ —
◇ —
♣ J 10 4

EAST
♠ —
♡ Q J 9
◇ 10
♣ 9 3 2

SOUTH
♠ Q J 10 8
♡ —
◇ —
♣ 7 6 5

Dix led a club, and West played her jack. The declarer won with the king and ruffed a heart high, collecting another underruff. This scenario was repeated: a club to the ace, with West unblocking the ten, and another heart ruffed high and underruffed.

South still had the faint hope that West had the club nine. But when he led his last club, East produced that card and West finally made her spade nine. To achieve that result, and a three-trick defeat, she underruffed three times, unblocked three times, and ruffed her partner's ace—one of the most remarkable series of defensive plays ever recorded.

July 1, 1983

TEST YOURSELF

A famous authority on the game once stated that defense is the hardest part of the game. Great defenders, he suggested, are very much rarer than great bidders. Although this is an arguable thesis, it is certainly true that the average player is less skilled in defense than in other areas: The problems are of a varied nature, and the literature available to the student is very limited.

Those who fancy their defensive skill should cover the South and East hands in the diagram, and study the problem that faces West after the fourth trick. He is defending four spades after the bidding shown and has led the heart king. South has won with the ace, cashed the ace–king of trumps, and led the heart ten for West to win. East has played high-low in hearts, and produced the three and nine of spades.

The problem was originated by a French analyst, Antoine Roux, and was forwarded to this writer by José le Dentu, one of the world's greatest bridge writers. As he mischievously sent just the problem, it is to be hoped that our solutions coincide.

Both West and North had some bidding problems. West decided that his hand was too good for a simple overcall of two hearts and elected to make a takeout double in the hope of bidding hearts later.

North's pass of the double was questionable. He could have made life easier for his partner by bidding one notrump.

When East responded to the double with two clubs, South jumped aggressively to three spades, and North lifted him to game. After winning the first trick with the heart ace and cashing two top spades, South gave up a heart to West, who was now looking at this position:

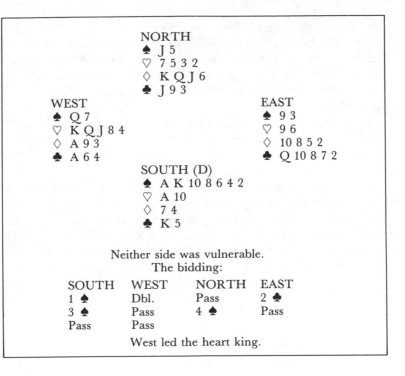

NORTH
♠ J 5
♡ 7 5 3 2
◇ K Q J 6
♣ J 9 3

WEST
♠ Q 7
♡ K Q J 8 4
◇ A 9 3
♣ A 6 4

EAST
♠ 9 3
♡ 9 6
◇ 10 8 5 2
♣ Q 10 8 7 2

SOUTH (D)
♠ A K 10 8 6 4 2
♡ A 10
◇ 7 4
♣ K 5

Neither side was vulnerable.
The bidding:

SOUTH	WEST	NORTH	EAST
1 ♠	Dbl.	Pass	2 ♣
3 ♠	Pass	4 ♠	Pass
Pass	Pass		

West led the heart king.

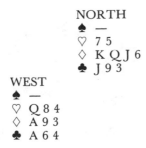

NORTH
♠ —
♡ 7 5
◇ K Q J 6
♣ J 9 3

WEST
♠ —
♡ Q 8 4
◇ A 9 3
♣ A 6 4

West can now piece together some facts, some inferences, and some assumptions. All the hearts are accounted for, and he knows that South began with a doubleton. It is virtually sure that South has all the remaining spades. If East has the spade ten, South has overbid and misplayed, and the contract will surely fail.

If South began with nine cards in the major suits, he must have four cards in the minor suits. And three of them must be losers for the defense to have a chance.

If South has three or four diamonds, his contract is safe. West can neglect that possibility. Can South have a singleton diamond? No, because East would then have five and would have bid two diamonds rather than two clubs in response to the double. So West is left with the possibility that South has a doubleton in each minor suit. If he has the king-queen of clubs, he will have no trouble.

By piecing together fragments of information and making some judicious assumptions, West has focused on the crucial situation. He has to plan a winning defense if South has a doubleton diamond and a doubleton king of clubs.

At this stage in a real game West could see that a low diamond lead, away from the ace, could do no harm and might do some good. It would force South to use his entry at once.

This is the right answer, but to prove it consider what would happen to West if he routinely led a heart winner at the fifth trick. South would ruff and cash two more trump winners:

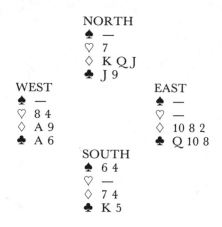

NORTH
♠ —
♡ 7
◇ K Q J
♣ J 9

WEST
♠ —
♡ 8 4
◇ A 9
♣ A 6

EAST
♠ —
♡ —
◇ 10 8 2
♣ Q 10 8

SOUTH
♠ 6 4
♡ —
◇ 7 4
♣ K 5

Another trump is led, and West is in trouble. If he throws a minor-suit card, South can lead that suit to establish his tenth trick. So West throws a heart, and South leads a diamond. West must duck, and South wins in the dummy and ruffs a heart with his last trump. Then a diamond lead endplays West, and the club king wins the last trick.

Now do you believe that defense is difficult?

MARCH 31, 1974

5
♥

LAWS AND ETHICS

Players in a home game frequently need to consult the laws of the game but seldom have a copy available. In tournament play it is simpler, for a director is on hand to give rulings. The list of problems that he must deal with is a long one, and some of them are quite obscure. Some of the commonest are hesitations, leads out of turn, and bids out of turn, which are featured in the next three deals. The fourth deal illustrates the dangers involved in trying to settle a problem without calling the director. And the fifth describes some outright confusion that is never likely to be repeated.

HESITATION LITIGATION

A wide field of complaint, in rubber bridge as well as duplicate play, is the inference from speed or lack of speed. An experienced player can often make sound, and illegitimate, deductions, consciously or subconsciously. If the partner bids or passes instantaneously, his action is clear-cut. If he hesitates, some alternative was available.

Players in New York tournaments are urged to pause before taking action in certain situations: first, before taking any action during the first round of bidding; second, before doubling or redoubling at any time; third, before making an opening lead; and fourth, before following to the first trick, if the declarer plays quickly from dummy.

Players who cultivate a good "tempo" in this way are less likely to generate suspicion, which would otherwise be the case. Consider the following opening lead problem:

♠ 10 8 5
♡ Q 9 6 2
◇ 9 8 5 3 2
♣ 8

Your right-hand opponent has opened with one notrump and been raised to three notrump. A diamond is the obvious lead, but the fact that the opponents did not use the Stayman convention might suggest a major-suit lead.

Now consider what you would lead if your partner hesitated before passing three notrump. He is most unlikely to want to launch out at the four-level in the face of such bidding, so presumably he was thinking of doubling.

In this situation a double has a commonsense conventional meaning: If you find the right lead, partner, we can defeat this contract. The inference is that the doubler has a long solid suit, and the leader will tend to lead his shortest suit. If the opponents both bid notrump, your short suit will tend to be your partner's long suit.

When this situation occurred in the Eastern Regionals, the opening lead was a club. This was a dramatic success because

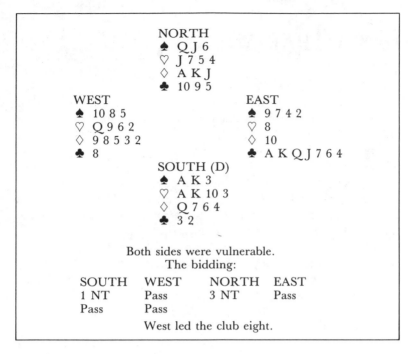

NORTH
♠ Q J 6
♡ J 7 5 4
◇ A K J
♣ 10 9 5

WEST
♠ 10 8 5
♡ Q 9 6 2
◇ 9 8 5 3 2
♣ 8

EAST
♠ 9 7 4 2
♡ 8
◇ 10
♣ A K Q J 7 6 4

SOUTH (D)
♠ A K 3
♡ A K 10 3
◇ Q 7 6 4
♣ 3 2

Both sides were vulnerable.
The bidding:

SOUTH	WEST	NORTH	EAST
1 NT	Pass	3 NT	Pass
Pass	Pass		

West led the club eight.

the complete deal was as shown.

The club lead defeated the contract by three tricks. With any other lead, at least nine tricks would have been made. The protest committee disallowed the lead, judging that West might have been influenced by his partner's hesitation.

Whether he actually was influenced, of course, is not subject to proof. If a player might have been influenced, an adjustment is usually made in the score.

If East had had the courage of his convictions and doubled, the club lead would have been entirely legitimate and East–West would have had a top score. Alternatively, the new policy of pausing could have helped. This was the first round of bidding, and if East had been able to restrict his thinking to three or four seconds, no inference would have been possible.

At other tables, North–South sometimes bid to four hearts, which was a sounder contract than three notrump. Four hearts could not be beaten, provided South took the precaution of ruffing the third round of clubs with a high trump. The ten was the obvious card for this purpose, but the ace or king also led to success.

June 19, 1966

LAY A TRAP AND CATCH YOURSELF

The danger lurking in the deal shown, from the writer's angle, is that readers will inspect the diagram and the bidding, draw a plausible but inaccurate conclusion, and turn disgustedly to another section of the paper or hurriedly pen a letter of indignant complaint to the editor on the subject of typography. Before taking either of these precipitate actions, the reader should ask himself what could possibly cause East to pass originally with 14 high-card points and a strong six-card major suit, and what could possibly cause South to open three notrump with a nondescript 13 points.

North and South had begun the day, in a regional pairs championship, by suffering a penalty of 500 points. While brooding on this misfortune, South opened the next hand with one club—only to be told that it was not his deal. His bid was canceled, the bidding reverted to West, and the unfortunate North was now condemned to silence throughout the auction.

When a player with an opening bid or better faces a partner who is required to pass, science goes out the window and psychology is the name of the game for both sides. The wretch who created this insoluble problem by his inattention usually takes a stab at three notrump, since this is the commonest of all contracts. The stab is more attractive if one or both opponents have passed, since this apparently increases the chance that the silenced partner has a good hand.

This clue was deceptive in this case, because Brian Glubok, a talented young expert from White Plains, New York, contributed a psychological pass in the East seat: A normal opening of one spade would have discouraged South, and Glubok had no wish to do that.

South accordingly stabbed at three notrump, and East happily doubled. He was less happy with the result. He had maneuvered South into a terrible contract, but it succeeded. A normal opening lead of a diamond would have given the defense the first five tricks, but West decided to play "safe" by leading the heart jack. This did not give away anything in the suit, but it gave South a chance to make the contract. And he took it.

The heart ace won the first trick, and the declarer had to hope for eight tricks in the black suits, five in clubs and three in spades.

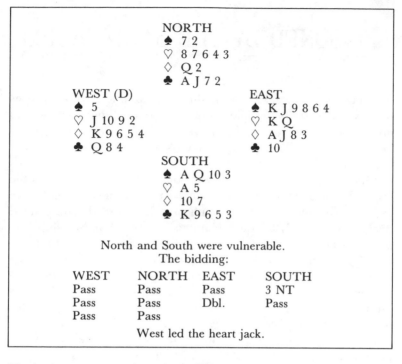

NORTH
♠ 7 2
♡ 8 7 6 4 3
♢ Q 2
♣ A J 7 2

WEST (D)
♠ 5
♡ J 10 9 2
♢ K 9 6 5 4
♣ Q 8 4

EAST
♠ K J 9 8 6 4
♡ K Q
♢ A J 8 3
♣ 10

SOUTH
♠ A Q 10 3
♡ A 5
♢ 10 7
♣ K 9 6 5 3

North and South were vulnerable.
The bidding:

WEST	NORTH	EAST	SOUTH
Pass	Pass	Pass	3 NT
Pass	Pass	Dbl.	Pass
Pass	Pass		

West led the heart jack.

He had to assume that the missing spade honors were on his right, so he decided to play for the club queen to be on his left.

Without even taking the simple precaution of playing the club king, thereby guarding against a singleton queen on his right, South led to the club jack. When this finesse succeeded, he tried the double finesse in spades by leading to the ten. It was then an easy matter to run clubs, repeating the spade finesse en route, to take nine tricks.

If any of the three key black cards had been misplaced for him. South's improbable contract would have failed by five tricks, for a penalty of 1,400 points.

Glubok and his partner were undeterred by this disaster, and went on to win the Open Pair title. There were two silver linings: They had broken even on the round; and they had a very sad story to tell to anyone who would listen.

SEPTEMBER 25, 1977

POISONED BY THE SANDWICHES

The laws of bridge have something in common with its techniques. They are both highly complex, nobody knows everything about them, and there are always new situations that have not been thought of. The average player is relatively ignorant in both areas and often pays the price.

One of the commonest irregularities at the bridge table is the exposure of a card by a defender. But few players below the expert level understand the applicable law. On the diagramed deal, from the 1979 Grand National Team Championship, the players were expert and knew their rights. East–West found that they had been sandwiched with disastrous consequences.

South's pre-emptive opening of three hearts crowded the auction for everyone, and East–West climbed to six clubs. East was far from sure that he could make a slam, but he expected his opponents to sacrifice and they did so.

Since there are two quick losers in six clubs, the save was a phantom. Six hearts doubled was headed for a two-trick defeat, but an odd thing happened.

After West had led the club king and the trick had been quitted, a large order of sandwiches arrived for everyone. When the sandwiches had been sorted out, West, with his mind now in his stomach, led the diamond deuce under the delusion that he had won the first trick. The fact that South had ruffed had not registered.

The law was duly explained by the director, and South had the option of accepting the lead. Naturally, this did not suit him, and the diamond remained as a penalty card, to be played at the first legal opportunity. But there was more to it than that, as shortly appeared.

South cashed the heart queen, drawing both missing trumps, and took a spade finesse. East won his king and would have shifted to diamonds had the heavy hand of the law not intervened.

As West's diamond deuce was still on the table, South had the right to require or forbid a diamond lead. Naturally, he barred a diamond play, and the doubled slam was made. All the diamonds in the closed hand disappeared on dummy's spades.

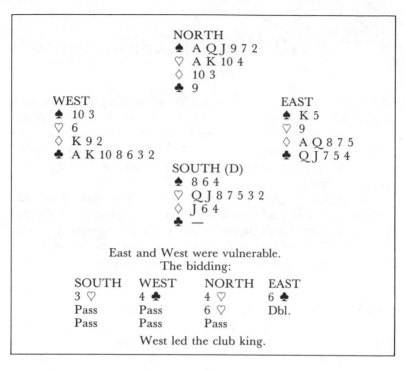

NORTH
♠ A Q J 9 7 2
♡ A K 10 4
◇ 10 3
♣ 9

WEST
♠ 10 3
♡ 6
◇ K 9 2
♣ A K 10 8 6 3 2

EAST
♠ K 5
♡ 9
◇ A Q 8 7 5
♣ Q J 7 5 4

SOUTH (D)
♠ 8 6 4
♡ Q J 8 7 5 3 2
◇ J 6 4
♣ —

East and West were vulnerable.
The bidding:

SOUTH	WEST	NORTH	EAST
3 ♡	4 ♣	4 ♡	6 ♣
Pass	Pass	6 ♡	Dbl.
Pass	Pass	Pass	

West led the club king.

It is not clear that South was right to draw trumps immediately, for it might have given West a chance to discard his fatal penalty card. This episode was reported in mingled rage and sadness by Marge Gwozdzinsky of New York.

She held the North cards in the replay and did the right thing by refusing to save over six clubs. This would have gained 9 international match points in normal circumstances, but the actual result was a loss of 15. The sandwiches had cost her team 24 points, a massive swing in a close district semifinal match.

SEPTEMBER 17, 1980

AD HOC DECISION

Bridge players en masse are about as law-abiding, no more and no less, than the general public: A tiny minority deliberately flouts the law; a larger minority meticulously observes both the laws and the proprieties; and in between is a large group that commits small misdemeanors, either through ignorance or because punishment seems unlikely.

Tournament players frequently flout, often with disastrous consequences, one particular law. It states that players are obliged to call the tournament director whenever any irregularity occurs at the table. Many players feel that they know the law and that they can settle matters among themselves. But they don't and they can't, as many examples have demonstrated.

A poignant instance occurred in 1984 at one of the world's great tournaments, the Caransa-Mai in Amsterdam. It invariably attracts many top-ranked teams from all parts of Europe, and on this occasion was won by a Polish team.

South might have passed in the fourth seat on the diagramed deal, and if he had there would have been no story. But his bidding methods included a weak notrump and he used it. North responded with a Stayman two-club bid, intending to raise hearts or play diamonds. This would not have worked out very well, but West unwisely entered the auction by doubling two diamonds, which was South's denial of a major suit.

This seemed a desirable contract to North, and he announced this with a redouble. He was surprised and pleased when everyone stood their ground. East had considerable misgivings, but trusted his partner.

West made the eccentric lead of the spade eight, and South won with the ace. He led to the heart ace and played the club eight to his jack. This forced the ace, and the defense persevered with spades. South ruffed in dummy, cashed the heart king, and exited with a heart. West won and led the club three, allowing the declarer to discard dummy's remaining heart and win in his hand in this position:

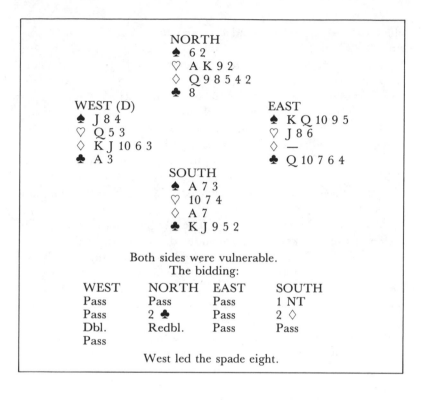

NORTH
♠ 6 2
♡ A K 9 2
♢ Q 9 8 5 4 2
♣ 8

WEST (D)
♠ J 8 4
♡ Q 5 3
♢ K J 10 6 3
♣ A 3

EAST
♠ K Q 10 9 5
♡ J 8 6
♢ —
♣ Q 10 7 6 4

SOUTH
♠ A 7 3
♡ 10 7 4
♢ A 7
♣ K J 9 5 2

Both sides were vulnerable.
The bidding:

WEST	NORTH	EAST	SOUTH
Pass	Pass	Pass	1 NT
Pass	2 ♣	Pass	2 ♢
Dbl.	Redbl.	Pass	Pass
Pass			

West led the spade eight.

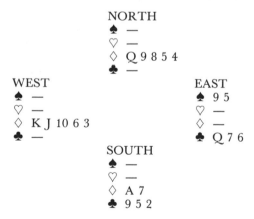

NORTH
♠ —
♡ —
♢ Q 9 8 5 4
♣ —

WEST
♠ —
♡ —
♢ K J 10 6 3
♣ —

EAST
♠ 9 5
♡ —
♢ —
♣ Q 7 6

SOUTH
♠ —
♡ —
♢ A 7
♣ 9 5 2

South cashed the diamond ace and was not surprised to find
all the trumps on his left. He was now safe for his contract, but
he became careless: He led the club nine and directed his partner
to play "small." A split-second later he realized that West had

played the diamond ten and changed his instruction to "over-ruff."

East and West accepted this, in the mistaken belief that a correction "in the same breath" was legal. North–South scored 710, and East–West went away and talked to a director. They discovered, a little late, that the overruff would have been barred if the director had been called as he should have been: South may amend a verbal slip, but not to change his mind.

The East–West team asked for an adjustment, suggesting that either they should score 400, as they would have done if the director had been called, or a redeal, or a complete cancellation of the deal.

North was René Ducheyne of The Hague, Netherlands, who is one of the best-known personalities of the world bridge scene. As captain of his team, he had an ethical problem. Legally he was on strong ground, since the director had not been called in time. But he recognized that there was a moral claim, and he did not wish to accept a score of minus 400. So he accepted the suggestion that the deal be canceled completely, without knowing what had happened earlier to his teammates.

He explained all this when he compared scores with his East–West pair. "You did what?" they screamed. "You canceled it? Against us, they played five diamonds doubled. We scored 1,100 and you canceled it!"

July 7, 1985

TOTAL CONFUSION FOR PLAYERS, DIRECTOR, AND COMMITTEE

A Vanderbilt Knockout match between teams led by Edith Kemp and Andrew Bernstein generated the most wildly complicated chain of events ever brought before an appeals committee. Bernstein and Steve Altman of New York held the West and East hands, respectively, and were members of a four-man team exhausted by days of continuous play. Their opponents were Clifford Russell of Miami Beach, sitting South, and Mrs. Kemp, sitting North.

Russell chose to pass the freak South hand in second position, and Bernstein opened the West hand with one diamond. The response of two clubs was overcalled with two spades, and West's pass was based on a partnership understanding that East must bid again in such a situation.

North raised to three spades, and at this point the confusion began.

One of the players, probably North but possibly South, asked for a review of the auction. Bernstein gave a review, but gave the opening bid as a one notrump instead of one diamond. This was a slip of which he was quite unaware, but it naturally worried his partner quite considerably.

Altman, therefore, asked for a review in his turn, and Mrs. Kemp repeated the erroneous sequence with the one notrump opening bid. This satisfied everybody except Bernstein, who was not listening, and Altman, who turned scarlet and seemed about to be taken ill.

Mrs. Kemp suggested that they break for five minutes so that Altman could recover. But he insisted on continuing, and needed a walk around the room, a glass of water, and eight minutes' thought before he could decide what to do.

His problem was not a technical one: He did not know whether he should explain that his previous bid had been made under the "delusion" that the opening was one diamond. As everyone else seemed satisfied that the opening bid was one notrump, he concluded that he had misheard his partner. He eventually decided

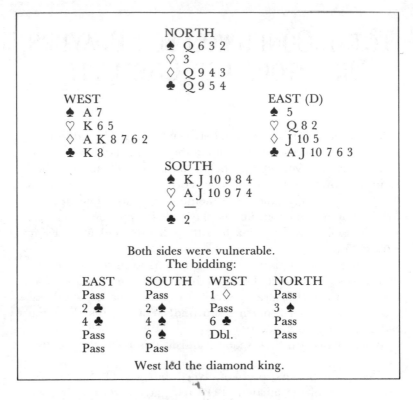

NORTH
♠ Q 6 3 2
♡ 3
◇ Q 9 4 3
♣ Q 9 5 4

WEST
♠ A 7
♡ K 6 5
◇ A K 8 7 6 2
♣ K 8

EAST (D)
♠ 5
♡ Q 8 2
◇ J 10 5
♣ A J 10 7 6 3

SOUTH
♠ K J 10 9 8 4
♡ A J 10 9 7 4
◇ —
♣ 2

Both sides were vulnerable.
The bidding:

EAST	SOUTH	WEST	NORTH
Pass	Pass	1 ◇	Pass
2 ♣	2 ♠	Pass	3 ♠
4 ♣	4 ♠	6 ♣	Pass
Pass	6 ♠	Dbl.	Pass
Pass	Pass		

West led the diamond king.

that he should say nothing, because any explanation would give improper information about his hand, and bid four clubs.

At this point Russell asked Altman to leave the table while he asked Bernstein a question. Altman left, and Mrs. Kemp decided that she should leave also. Russell then asked Bernstein whether the two-club bid had been Stayman.

Bernstein was astonished by the question, because he knew that he had opened one diamond and was unaware that he himself and Mrs. Kemp had both given one notrump as the opening.

The two missing players then returned, and they all asked one of the spectators what the bidding had been. The answer was: "Would you like the bidding as it actually went or as it was reviewed?"

This dispelled the confusion, and the players chose to continue without calling a tournament director.

Over four clubs South bid four spades, and West made a surprising jump to six clubs. This contract could have been defeated by three tricks, for a penalty of 800 points, but South continued to six spades and was down one, losing a trick in each black suit.

At this point Mrs. Kemp decided to call the tournament director and lodge a protest. He ruled that a substitute deal should be played on a provisional basis. The Bernstein team played this under protest and lost 6 points on it.

On the original deal the Bernstein team gained 14 points by making five spades doubled in the other room, giving them a 17-point victory in the match.

The chief tournament director at first ruled that the original board should not count, in which case the substitute deal would give the Kemp team a 3-point win. He later changed his mind, but the whole matter was deferred for consideration by the appeals committee.

After a great deal of soul-searching, the committee ruled that the original result should stand, so the Bernstein team survived to play another day.

August 7, 1967

6

HISTORY

We start this section with Harold Vanderbilt's famous cruise, the turning point in the history of bridge. But we are more concerned with world history, which has often involved the game: Winston Churchill played auction while waiting for the outbreak of World War I; and General Dwight Eisenhower played while waiting for news of the landings in North Africa.

The second item is an anachronism from the France of the Bourbons. The third concerns Vietnam before it acquired that unhappy name. The fourth is a poignant episode from World War II. And finally, with a deal that was named "Hand of the Year" by the International Bridge Press Association, we are in modern China, striding toward prosperity under the guidance of some bridge enthusiasts.

CRUISING
FROM AUCTION TO CONTRACT

The exact date on which contract bridge in its modern form was born during Harold Vanderbilt's famous cruise through the Panama Canal was long in some doubt. It now turns out to be Halloween 1925 aboard the liner *Finland.*

Vanderbilt and three of his friends, Frederic S. Allen, Francis M. Bacon 3rd, and Dudley Pickman, Jr., began experimenting when the Finland reached Balboa. The ship could not proceed until daylight, but the passengers were not allowed ashore and a historic game began.

Building on the plafond idea, which required the players to bid to their "ceiling," Vanderbilt improvised a new scoring table that allowed for large slam bonuses and the vulnerability factor. The term "vulnerable" was contributed by another passenger, a young woman who had tried to interest the foursome in a complicated Oriental card game.

Brief tests of the new game were made on the last leg of the voyage to Havana and proved satisfactory. On returning home Vanderbilt passed copies of the rules to a few friends, and contract bridge spread rapidly in the clubs of New York and New England.

On the following deal Bacon got the better of his mentor, Vanderbilt, who drew a logical inference only to find his calculations upset by a lead-inhibiting bid, one of the earliest on record.

Bacon, sitting South, felt slam-minded when his partner raised to three spades. This was before the day of Blackwood, or even of cue-bidding to show controls, and the four-club bid was a deceptive maneuver aimed at stopping a club lead. The chief danger from South's viewpoint was that the defense might be able to cash two immediate club tricks.

When four clubs was raised to five clubs, Vanderbilt, who was West, not unnaturally assumed that both his opponents held club length. His double was based on the expectation that East held a singleton or void club and would set the contract with a ruff.

It seemed likely to South that his partner, who had cooperated in the move toward slam, held two aces and some club strength.

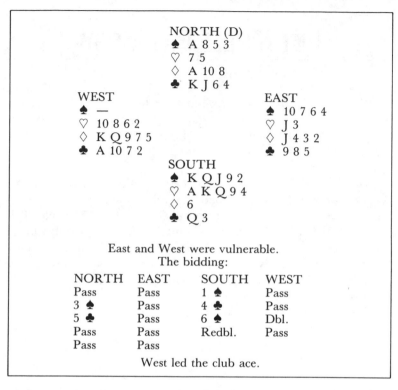

NORTH (D)
♠ A 8 5 3
♡ 7 5
◇ A 10 8
♣ K J 6 4

WEST
♠ —
♡ 10 8 6 2
◇ K Q 9 7 5
♣ A 10 7 2

EAST
♠ 10 7 6 4
♡ J 3
◇ J 4 3 2
♣ 9 8 5

SOUTH
♠ K Q J 9 2
♡ A K Q 9 4
◇ 6
♣ Q 3

East and West were vulnerable.
The bidding:

NORTH	EAST	SOUTH	WEST
Pass	Pass	1 ♠	Pass
3 ♠	Pass	4 ♣	Pass
5 ♣	Pass	6 ♠	Dbl.
Pass	Pass	Redbl.	Pass
Pass	Pass		

West led the club ace.

His redouble was based on sound mathematics: It stood to gain 360 points if the contract was made and to lose 100 if the result was a one-trick set, odds of almost four to one.

After the lead of the ace and another club, South did not even need to ruff a heart. He could draw all the trumps and discard his two low hearts on dummy's clubs.

If North–South had not bid clubs, West's natural lead would have been the diamond king. South would then have been slightly embarrassed by the bad trump split and forced to try for a heart ruff before drawing all of East's trumps.

East could have given him a nasty moment by false-carding with the jack on the first heart lead, but the declarer would have had no alternative to continuing with hearts. The third round would be ruffed with the spade ace, and the spade nine finessed on the next trick.

December 26, 1965

LET THEM EAT CROW

Getting rid of a king who is blocking the road to liberty is a revolutionary proceeding that may be as necessary in bridge as it is in history. The diagramed deal, forwarded by Captain Edgar Peixotto, living appropriately on the Boulevard du Roi, Versailles, France, proves the point.

As this deal has a very long history, going back before the days of contract bridge, a modest exercise of anachronistic imagination can set the scene in the French Court in 1789. North is the ill-fated Louis XVI, well-meaning but weak. South is Queen Marie Antoinette, beautiful but poorly educated and shockingly extravagant. West is a soldier who believes in showing his strength. And East is a courtier who knows that he should not intervene in a royal dialogue.

The science of bidding was in a primitive state in those far-off days, but this does not entirely explain the strange North–South bidding. We must do a little mind-reading.

The King: "This is a great hand. I suppose I could show it by a cue-bid of two clubs. But Marie might think I have a club suit, and I should hate to have to play two clubs. A takeout double seems my safest move."

The Queen: "I'm glad I've got Louis into a bridge game. Perhaps it'll take his mind off his troubles with the Estates-General. This looks like a good hand and I suppose I had better bid hearts. I think he could pass two hearts, so I'll bid three hearts."

The King: "I wonder what she means by that. It should be pre-emptive, but I'm not sure she is up to that. If she has a good hand she might not think of making a cue-bid of two clubs, but I don't see how she can be strong with the hand I've got when West has bid twice. I'll just bid four hearts."

The Queen: "I have a feeling that old pessimist over there has more than he has shown me. I have control of all the side suits, and I like bidding slams. Let's surprise them. Seven hearts."

The King: *"Mon Dieu!"*

The Queen: "The impertinence of that old marshal, doubling me! I expect he has the heart king and thinks it is a trick. Won't he be surprised to see the ace in the dummy? I redouble on principle."

```
                        NORTH
                        ♠ A Q 8
                        ♡ A K Q J
                        ◇ Q J 10 9 8 2
                        ♣ —
      WEST (D)                             EAST
      ♠ K J 10 9                           ♠ 7 6 5 4 3 2
      ♡ 9 8 6 4                            ♡ —
      ◇ —                                  ◇ 7 6 5 4 3
      ♣ K Q J 9 6                          ♣ 10 5
                        SOUTH
                        ♠ —
                        ♡ 10 7 5 3 2
                        ◇ A K
                        ♣ A 8 7 4 3 2
```

Both sides were vulnerable.
The bidding:

WEST	NORTH	EAST	SOUTH
1 ♣	Dbl.	Pass	3 ♡
3 ♠	4 ♡	Pass	7 ♡
Dbl.	Pass	Pass	Redbl.
Pass	Pass	Pass	

West led the club king.

Louis laid down his cards and said, "I think you'll like the dummy, my dear."

The Queen: "Oh, thank you, Louis. It's a lovely dummy and I'm going to make it easily. Let me see. I will have five trump tricks, six diamonds, and two black aces. Nothing to it. I will discard a spade from dummy, win with the ace of clubs, and draw trumps."

But Marie had a surprise on the second trick when East played a spade on the first round of trumps. The easy slam was not so easy after all. Then she saw a ray of daylight.

"I'm not dead yet. I can ruff the queen of spades, cash the king of diamonds, and draw trumps. Then I can discard the diamond ace on the spade ace—a beautiful play—and make the diamonds in dummy."

She tried this plan, but West ruffed the king of diamonds.

The Queen: "It's not fair! *He* didn't have any trumps, and now *you* haven't any diamonds. It was a beautiful slam, and it was ruined by that *silly* distribution. I hate bridge! I'm not going to play anymore!"

She left the room in mounting hysteria, followed closely by the King. East and West discussed the deal.

"I wouldn't have dared to tell her," remarked the courtier, a good bridge player as well as the soul of tact, "but she should have made it.

"Let me show you, *mon vieux*. The idea is to get the closed hand with one fewer trump than the open. She should have discarded a diamond from dummy at the first trick, not a spade. Then she can win in her hand with the club ace, lead a trump to dummy, and ruff a spade. Another trump lead and another spade ruff leaves the queen with one trump and dummy with two. Then she can draw trumps, discarding the ace of diamonds, and then get rid of the king of diamonds on the spade ace.

"It is sad for France that the royal family does not have any foresight. The Bourbons cannot conceive that it might be right to get rid of a king."

November 3, 1968

WHEN KINGS WERE ACES

A number of heads of state, including the late President Eisenhower and several kings and queens of the three-dimensional variety, have been bridge enthusiasts. Two of them have a major place in the legend and literature of the game. One was the Emir of Afghanistan, Amanullah II, who had to abdicate in 1929 because his Moslem subjects disapproved, among other things, of his playing cards, which showed the human form. The other was the Emperor Bao-Dai of Annam, who became the hero of the unique deal shown in the diagram.

This was many years before his hereditary dominions became an unhappy focus of world attention under the changed name of Vietnam, but he had numerous problems to face and the cares of government weighed heavily upon him. After a hard day at the Imperial Palace at Dalat, during which he had had a violent disagreement with his chief minister, he sat down to play in the East position. And the chief minister was his partner.

After both sides had scored a game, the governmental duo had a slight misfortune: They bid too much on a misfit hand, went down 1,100 points, and were therefore even more irritated with each other, and more inclined to be cautious, when the diagramed deal came along.

After South passed, West bid a cautious three clubs. He had something in hand for this, since the same bid would have been appropriate with one club fewer. But none of the possible alternatives—pass, one club, or four clubs—was completely satisfactory.

The emperor had been looking forward to playing a four-heart contract, or perhaps even a slam, and was disgusted to learn from the opening bid that his partner held nothing but long, strong clubs. He therefore retired into his tent and remained silent for the whole auction, a slightly strange decision that proved to be justified. If he had played in four hearts doubled, perfect defense, starting with a trump lead, could have beaten him three tricks for a penalty of 800.

North's bidding left a good deal to be desired. His double of three clubs was meant for penalties, and he should certainly have passed on the next round when South retreated to three dia-

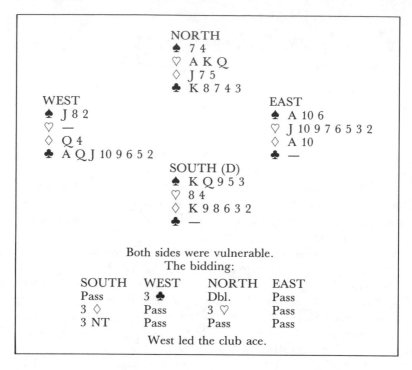

NORTH
♠ 7 4
♡ A K Q
◇ J 7 5
♣ K 8 7 4 3

WEST
♠ J 8 2
♡ —
◇ Q 4
♣ A Q J 10 9 6 5 2

EAST
♠ A 10 6
♡ J 10 9 7 6 5 3 2
◇ A 10
♣ —

SOUTH (D)
♠ K Q 9 5 3
♡ 8 4
◇ K 9 8 6 3 2
♣ —

Both sides were vulnerable.
The bidding:

SOUTH	WEST	NORTH	EAST
Pass	3 ♣	Dbl.	Pass
3 ◇	Pass	3 ♡	Pass
3 NT	Pass	Pass	Pass

West led the club ace.

monds. However, he surprised East with a bid of three hearts, aiming at three notrump, and South felt himself on strong ground in making that bid in spite of the apparent misfit.

A glance at the North–South cards suggests that three notrump is a shaky contract, but a closer look at the four hands reveals that the cards lie very well for the declarer. West has no side entry for his clubs, and both diamonds and spades develop favorably if they are led from the North hand. In fact South seems bound to succeed, a development hardly calculated to improve the imperial temper.

West decided that he might as well establish his clubs and hope that the diamond queen or the spade jack would prove to be an entry. He led the club ace, and when dummy followed, the emperor glared savagely around the table and produced the diamond ace. Such was the force of his personality that nobody at the table said a word, although a few kibitzing courtiers raised a delicate eyebrow.

West continued with the club queen, and South put on the king. Glaring around him once more, the emperor discarded the spade ace. At this point the kibitzers left in a body and huddled in a corner, whispering.

"He's throwing away all of his aces—he must have gone mad," was the general theory, although a minority held that the emperor was simply determined to make his partner lose. When they returned to the table, the emperor had left hurriedly to give orders for the quelling of a provincial rebellion. They inquired about the result and found that South had gone down two tricks. What was more, there was no way in which he could have done better.

An extended postmortem revealed that the contract would have been made against any normal defense, using either the spades or the diamonds, since West could be kept out of the lead. If East had contended himself with just one spectacular ace discard, the other suit would have furnished enough tricks.

Nobody ever dared to ask the emperor to explain the reasoning behind his remarkable defense, but it has been known ever since as the Emperor's Coup.

MARCH 25, 1973

OPENING LEAD DELAYED
BY NAZIS

At the 1984 World Team Olympiad in Seattle, two leading Dutch bridge personalities were able to swap stories about old bad times.

One was Hans Kreyns, a former world pair champion who was captain of the Dutch women's team that took the bronze medal after dominating the qualifying play. The other was Evelyn Senn, who presented the annual Bols Brilliancy Prize on behalf of the world's oldest liqueur corporation.

The two were neighbors in Rotterdam forty years ago during the final desperate winter of World War II. The Allied armies had bypassed the northern parts of the Netherlands, and there was no heating and little food. Everyone counted the days until liberation, but it seemed slow in coming.

Bridge offered some escape from reality. Mrs. Senn, then Miss Gorter, had little interest, but her parents and her brother were enthusiasts. One memorable night they recruited as a fourth Mr. Boomers, the local butcher. He was virtually unemployed and planned to stay the night with his hosts to avoid a breach of the curfew.

Not unnaturally, Mrs. Senn does not recall the details of the crucial deal. The diagramed layout is therefore fictional, but the story and the finale are fact. The host and hostess, Dr. and Mrs. Gorter, bid briskly to slam, using a new American convention that they had learned from the Kreyns family.

East doubled, for no very good reason, and everything hinged on the opening lead. With East on lead, the normal situation in six diamonds, the slam would be unbeatable. But with West on lead, because of the artificial response to Blackwood, the heart lead shown in the diagram was due to give the defense the first four tricks and a penalty of 800, since the fourth heart lead from East allows West to score the diamond ten.

In the heat of the moment there was a distinct risk that the lead would come from the wrong side, making a difference of 2,290 points. And at this moment there was an interruption.

A platoon of German soldiers burst into the house and pointed guns at the four players. They were collecting local men for a

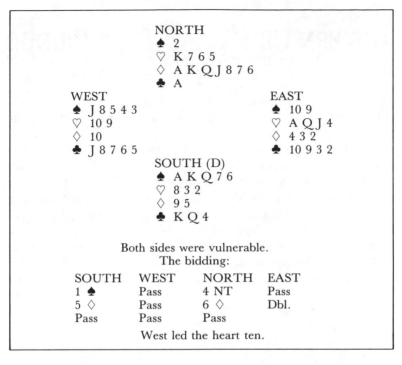

NORTH
- ♠ 2
- ♡ K 7 6 5
- ♢ A K Q J 8 7 6
- ♣ A

WEST
- ♠ J 8 5 4 3
- ♡ 10 9
- ♢ 10
- ♣ J 8 7 6 5

EAST
- ♠ 10 9
- ♡ A Q J 4
- ♢ 4 3 2
- ♣ 10 9 3 2

SOUTH (D)
- ♠ A K Q 7 6
- ♡ 8 3 2
- ♢ 9 5
- ♣ K Q 4

Both sides were vulnerable.
The bidding:

SOUTH	WEST	NORTH	EAST
1 ♠	Pass	4 NT	Pass
5 ♢	Pass	6 ♢	Dbl.
Pass	Pass	Pass	

West led the heart ten.

work project and examined everyone's papers. Dr. Gorter was exempt as a physician, and his son could prove that he had just returned with seriously impaired health from two years as a slave laborer in Berlin. But the soldiers took Mr. Boomers.

Dr. Gorter bravely followed them, found the German commanding officer, and argued on behalf of the unfortunate butcher: "He is my patient, and if he does not have these pills regularly he will be seriously ill."

Waving a bottle of aspirin proved sufficient to convince the German commander. Two hours after the interruption, the two men returned to the bridge table.

"Now," demanded Mr. Boomers, "whose lead is it?"

JANUARY 20, 1985

GOVERN CHINA AND PLAY BRIDGE

In preparation for President Reagan's 1984 visit to China, a New York bridge expert, Kathy Wei, was summoned to the White House to aid in briefing the President. Mrs. Wei, whose memoirs of a turbulent childhood in China are entitled *Second Daughter,* has had more direct contact with the top levels of Chinese government in this decade than almost any other American citizen. Her access has been via her skill at bridge, to which many Chinese officials, among them China's leader Deng Xiaoping, have long been devoted.

When Mrs. Wei was in Beijing on business for her husband, Charles Wei, a shipowner, she partnered Deputy Prime Minister Wan Li, designated to head the Chinese committee discussing nuclear energy problems. Wan, a bridge enthusiast, has a reputation at the bridge table, and away from it, for being energetic, clever, and unorthodox. He demonstrated the first two of these qualities on the diagramed deal.

The partnership was using the Precision System devised by Charles Wei and favored by most Chinese players. So one club was an artificial strong bid and West's double promised length in the major suits. One diamond by Mrs. Wei was also artificial, showing 6–7 high-card points, and the bidding then followed a natural track. The final redouble indicates Wan Li's aggressive optimism: The Chinese leaders seem psychologically inclined to redouble, which the American diplomats might bear in mind.

The West player was Ding Guangen, the vice-secretary-general of the People's Congress, and neither he nor his partner chose to retreat to five spades. That would have failed by just one trick, barring a misguess in trumps. Instead, he produced an imaginative lead of the spade eight. He was hoping to give his partner the lead for a heart return, and he chose the eight rather than a small card for suit-preference reasons. But South ruffed and studied his prospects. It was obvious that the hearts were on his left, and he was in considerable danger of losing three tricks in that suit.

Many players would charge ahead, supposing that they could strip out the side suits and eventually duck a heart to West. But Wan correctly saw that this would not quite work. By the time

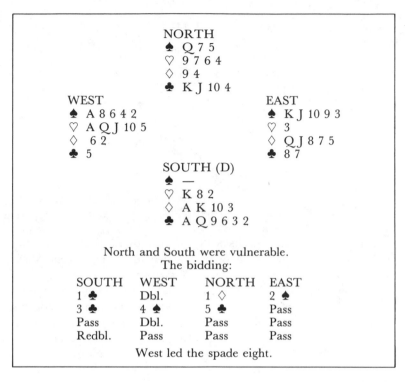

NORTH
♠ Q 7 5
♡ 9 7 6 4
♢ 9 4
♣ K J 10 4

WEST
♠ A 8 6 4 2
♡ A Q J 10 5
♢ 6 2
♣ 5

EAST
♠ K J 10 9 3
♡ 3
♢ Q J 8 7 5
♣ 8 7

SOUTH (D)
♠ —
♡ K 8 2
♢ A K 10 3
♣ A Q 9 6 3 2

North and South were vulnerable.
The bidding:

SOUTH	WEST	NORTH	EAST
1 ♣	Dbl.	1 ♢	2 ♠
3 ♣	4 ♠	5 ♣	Pass
Pass	Dbl.	Pass	Pass
Redbl.	Pass	Pass	Pass

West led the spade eight.

he had drawn trumps and ruffed two diamonds in the dummy, he would have no trumps left in the dummy and the endplay would fail.

The bidding had marked West with the major suits, and that greatly improved the chance of finding East with both missing diamond honors. So South crossed to dummy with a trump lead and led the diamond nine. The East player was S. T. Weng, a visiting New York businessman, and if he had covered, the ten would have been finessed subsequently. But he correctly played low, and when South did likewise, holding his breath, the nine held.

The declarer had to hope that West could not ruff the second round of diamonds. He led the remaining diamond from dummy and won with the king when East played the jack. Now the road to the endplay was clear. A trump lead to the dummy and a spade ruff left this ending:

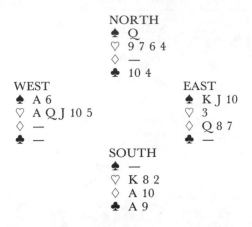

NORTH
♠ Q
♡ 9 7 6 4
◇ —
♣ 10 4

WEST
♠ A 6
♡ A Q J 10 5
◇ —
♣ —

EAST
♠ K J 10
♡ 3
◇ Q 8 7
♣ —

SOUTH
♠ —
♡ K 8 2
◇ A 10
♣ A 9

The spade queen was discarded on the diamond ace, and the diamond ten was ruffed. A heart was led to the eight, and West was forced to make a losing lead. Notice that the endplay would have been equally successful if East had held a singleton honor, for South would of course have played low. Wan had made his redoubled contract, and demonstrated the shrewdness and ability one would expect from a leader of the world's most populous country.

APRIL 29, 1984

7

PERSONALITIES

We begin with two deals about players who were involved in major matches in the 1930s: Harry St. John Ingram of England, who died in 1974 at the age of eighty-six, and Sophocles Venizelos, a member of the French team that played in the first world championship in 1937. Then we have a famous footballing Horse involved in a complex deal. The fourth deal concerns Barry Crane, owner of the world's biggest collection of master points, who was brutally murdered in his Hollywood home in 1985. Finally we star Omar Sharif, who has long been accustomed to a starring role.

WAS THIS PENALTY DOUBLE
A PSYCHIC?

In bridge, as in life, accidents resulting from momentary inattention may result in suffering for innocent parties. The diagramed deal, played in England, led to a North–South disaster after some strange bidding and generated some bewilderment that was only dissolved in the postmortem.

After two passes, East opened the bidding with three clubs. Such a bid would normally show a longer, stronger club suit and less outside strength, but undisciplined pre-emptive bids are permissible in the third seat when the fourth player can be assumed to have the best hand at the table.

South did have a strong hand and was somewhat inconvenienced by the three-club bid. An American player would probably double, a request for a takeout that is usually termed "optional," an inaccurate description.

But in England a double of a three-bid is treated as a penalty double. South therefore jumped to four spades, hoping that he would not find a dummy with a singleton spade and length in hearts.

West was Harry Ingram, an eighty-one-year-old player who came close to beating Ely Culbertson's team in the Schwab Cup match in 1934. He played extremely well all his life, notwithstanding the evidence of the double of four spades holding a virtually defenseless hand.

The opening lead of the club king was taken in the dummy with the ace, and South entered his hand with a diamond lead to the king. He felt convinced from the double that West had at least three spades headed by the king–jack, so he led to the spade queen in dummy.

To South's astonishment, East won with the spade king and returned his remaining diamond, a good play. The declarer overtook his diamond queen with the ace in dummy and tried to cash the diamond jack. East ruffed with the spade six and was overruffed.

South had to lose a second trump trick and two heart tricks,

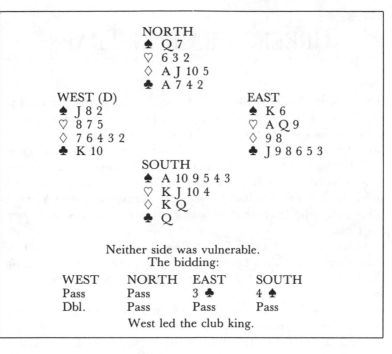

NORTH
♠ Q 7
♡ 6 3 2
◇ A J 10 5
♣ A 7 4 2

WEST (D)
♠ J 8 2
♡ 8 7 5
◇ 7 6 4 3 2
♣ K 10

EAST
♠ K 6
♡ A Q 9
◇ 9 8
♣ J 9 8 6 5 3

SOUTH
♠ A 10 9 5 4 3
♡ K J 10 4
◇ K Q
♣ Q

Neither side was vulnerable.
The bidding:

WEST	NORTH	EAST	SOUTH
Pass	Pass	3 ♣	4 ♠
Dbl.	Pass	Pass	Pass

West led the club king.

going one down. Indeed, he needed the three-three heart division to avoid going down two tricks.

Inspection of the traveling score slip showed that at other tables four spades undoubled had been made. The declarers had had no great difficulty after an opening lead in a red suit from West.

North–South were unhappy about their score, and East was puzzled.

"That was a brave double of yours, Harry," he remarked, "after I'd bid three clubs."

"Three clubs?" gasped Ingram. "I thought you bid two clubs."

SEPTEMBER 20, 1969

GREEKS BEARING TRAPS

The languid leader of Britain's famed Bloomsbury Group, Lyt- · ton Strachey, is quoted as saying that politics is no more than "a fairly adequate substitute for bridge." Whether this barb was aimed at the bridge players as well as the politicians is not clear.

What is clear is that statesmen have often been bridge players. Britain's Edward VII invariably played after dinner, but it is unlikely that he ever had to suffer a partnership with Winston Churchill, who in those days was a Liberal politician and a very poor player.

More recently Dwight David Eisenhower was the only American President with a passion for bridge. And Deng Xiaoping, the leader of China, plays into the small hours whenever he can manage it.

But there is no doubt whatever that the best bridge player among the statesmen and politicians was Sophocles Venizelos of Greece, who eventually followed in the footsteps of his famous father by becoming Prime Minister of his country. During a period of exile in France in the 1930s, he represented his adopted country on several occasions, winning the European team title in Brussels in 1935 and losing the first World Championship match later that year to the Four Aces in Madison Square Garden.

Making "unmakeable" contracts was his specialty, and he may have invented the "Coup de Venizelos" which he brought off on the diagramed deal. He was playing rubber bridge in Vichy against two Greek compatriots, and his admiring partner was the Grand Old Man of French bridge, Pierre Albarran.

The auction made use of Blackwood, then a newfangled idea which had made its way from Indianapolis to France. The contract appears to hinge on the diamond finesse, but it was clear to Venizelos that the finesse was going to lose: East had not only overcalled, but he had, rather foolishly, doubled six hearts. It was clear that he expected to score a trick with the diamond king.

West led a spade, and East took his ace. He then exited with his singleton trump and sat back in the confident expectation that he would score at least one of his well-placed minor-suit kings. But his confidence was somewhat shaken when Venizelos won

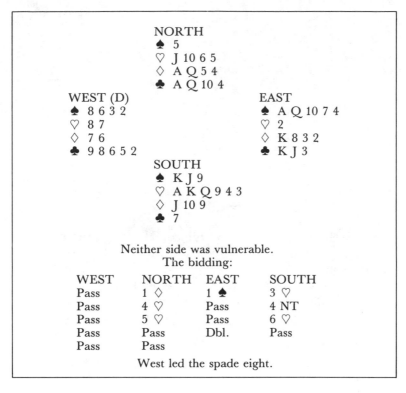

NORTH
♠ 5
♡ J 10 6 5
◇ A Q 5 4
♣ A Q 10 4

WEST (D)
♠ 8 6 3 2
♡ 8 7
◇ 7 6
♣ 9 8 6 5 2

EAST
♠ A Q 10 7 4
♡ 2
◇ K 8 3 2
♣ K J 3

SOUTH
♠ K J 9
♡ A K Q 9 4 3
◇ J 10 9
♣ 7

Neither side was vulnerable.
The bidding:

WEST	NORTH	EAST	SOUTH
Pass	1 ◇	1 ♠	3 ♡
Pass	4 ♡	Pass	4 NT
Pass	5 ♡	Pass	6 ♡
Pass	Pass	Dbl.	Pass
Pass	Pass		

West led the spade eight.

with the trump ace, led the diamond jack to dummy's ace, and played the diamond four.

East concluded that South had no more diamonds and was attempting to establish dummy's queen for a club discard. He therefore followed low, and realized that he had fallen into the trap when the ten won in the closed hand. But Venizelos still had work to do.

Taking his diamond pitcher to the well once more by leading from dummy toward the nine was unlikely to succeed because West had played the seven–six to show a doubleton. The club finesse seemed doomed, but there was a good chance for a squeeze (better than ruffing out the club king, although as it happens that would have succeeded). The declarer trumped his spade jack and ran major-suit winners to reach this position:

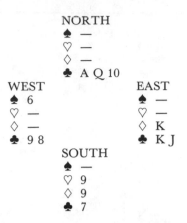

NORTH
♠ —
♡ —
◇ —
♣ A Q 10

WEST
♠ 6
♡ —
◇ —
♣ 9 8

EAST
♠ —
♡ —
◇ K
♣ K J

SOUTH
♠ —
♡ 9
◇ 9
♣ 7

On the last trump East was ruined. He let go the diamond king, and the diamond nine scored in the closed hand to bring home the slam.

The East–West players were sporting and friendly characters. They found the perfect way to compliment Venizelos for his brilliance by ordering a bottle of the best French champagne.

AUGUST 3, 1986

HORSING AROUND

Bridge is the only game or sport that people can—and do—play from the age of ten to the age of one hundred. Those who start by specializing in more vigorous activities have an opportunity to transfer their allegiance and often do so.

One example is Pauline Betz Addie of Bethesda, Maryland. She was the world's top-ranked woman tennis player in the 1940s, winning at Forest Hills and Wimbledon. She is a bridge enthusiast on a slightly lower level and has long been a life master.

Another is football star Alan Ameche, who won the Heisman Trophy in 1954. He was known as "The Horse" because of the way he plowed through opposing linemen and helped the Baltimore Colts win the National Football League title in 1958. Still competitive in a less energetic way, he helped the Overbrook Golf Club team, including Tom Rogers, Steve Dozer, and Edward Coterson, to win the 1981 Philadelphia Bridge Whist Association Team of Four Championship at the Cynwyd Club. One of the deals, shown in the diagram, was reported by Coterson and has a number of fascinating analytical points.

The reader who likes to analyze should study the diagram and try to answer three questions. One: What should the result be if South leads a spade against East's contract of five diamonds? Two: What should the result be if West leads a diamond against a contract of six hearts? Three: What should the result be if West leads a spade against six hearts?

At the first table North opened one spade and The Horse bid four diamonds with the East cards. South doubled and eventually doubled again after North had retreated to four spades and West had persevered to five diamonds.

The heart king was led, and the doubled game was made without difficulty. The spade shift was ruffed in the closed hand, and a heart was ruffed. A club was led, and it did not matter whether or not North took his ace, marked in his hand by the bidding and play to that point. The Horse could maneuver to ruff his remaining hearts and draw trump.

An opening spade lead, however, would have defeated the contract. East must surrender a heart to prepare for ruffs, and South can win and lead his remaining spade. If East attempts to

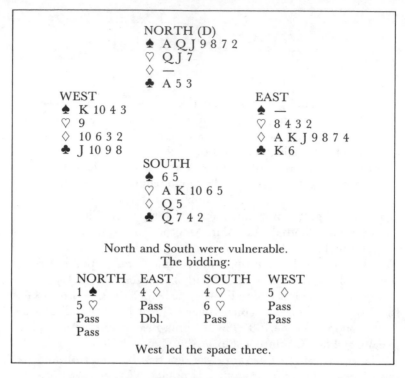

NORTH (D)
♠ A Q J 9 8 7 2
♡ Q J 7
♢ —
♣ A 5 3

WEST
♠ K 10 4 3
♡ 9
♢ 10 6 3 2
♣ J 10 9 8

EAST
♠ —
♡ 8 4 3 2
♢ A K J 9 8 7 4
♣ K 6

SOUTH
♠ 6 5
♡ A K 10 6 5
♢ Q 5
♣ Q 7 4 2

North and South were vulnerable.
The bidding:

NORTH	EAST	SOUTH	WEST
1 ♠	4 ♢	4 ♡	5 ♢
5 ♡	Pass	6 ♡	Pass
Pass	Dbl.	Pass	Pass
Pass			

West led the spade three.

ruff all his hearts, South can eventually score his diamond queen. If and when the declarer leads a club from the dummy, North wins and plays another spade.

The club king was a significant card at this table, but was even more significant in the replay. The bidding began similarly, but South bid his hearts at the four-level and landed in six hearts, as shown in the diagram.

East contributed a Lightner double to ask for an unusual lead, in this case a spade. If North had retreated to six spades (as he thought of doing) the double would have backfired, for North would have made his slam by finessing the spade nine.

However, the bidding ended, and West duly led a spade. South finessed, and East ruffed and led a diamond. This was ruffed in dummy and trumps were drawn. Another spade finesse and a ruff of a spade established the suit, and the club ace was available as an entry.

The slam was thus made, but the postmortem showed that East had missed a chance for a Deschapelles Coup. If he returns the club king at the second trick, South has no counter, since his vital entry to the dummy is removed.

The defenders suggested that they could have succeeded with a diamond lead. South proved that he could still succeed after ruffing in dummy and leading a low club. If East puts up his king, West can eventually be squeezed in the black suits. East does better to play low and the queen wins. Now South must draw trumps and finesse the spade nine. The remaining diamond loser is thrown on the spade ace, and the spade queen is led. A club is discarded and the spade king is the only trick for the defense.

September 27, 1981

HE WHO GOES TO THE TELEPHONE MAY MISS A CLUE

When not producing and directing television dramas, Barry Crane added enthusiastically to the world's biggest collection of master points. His remarkable successes, especially in big fields, were due to a combination of sharp card-play and hyperactive bidding. For example:

It seems that a fan sat behind Crane at the start of a regional pair championship and watched him attentively and silently for fifty-one deals. With one deal remaining it was clear to Crane, sitting East, that he had yet another title in the bag. The opponent in the South seat was called to the telephone, and while he was absent the kibitzer opened his mouth for the first time.

"Mr. Crane," he volunteered. "I have watched you for fifty-one deals, and you have bid on everyone of them."

Crane was not particularly surprised by this news and was saved from having to comment by the return of South, who opened one notrump.

West passed, and North raised to six notrump and turned to his left. "It's your bid, Mr. Crane," he announced. After inspecting his yarborough carefully, our hero doubled in firm tones.

North remembered too late that his partner had not been present for the preliminary conversation and had a moment of foreboding.

West led the club nine. South was somewhat surprised to be doubled and more surprised when the dummy appeared—it was clear that Crane could not have anything approaching two likely tricks. Presumably he had at least two of the missing queens.

The routine line of play was to take a finesse in spades and if this failed, guess what to do in the red suits. South thought of a better play: Strip out the clubs, cash the ace–king of spades, and play a third spade. If the spades were split three–two the contract would now be guaranteed, since a defender who began with three spades headed by the queen would have to lead a red suit and give the declarer his twelfth trick.

South began on this track by winning the club ace and following with the spade ace and the remaining club winners. But then

```
                        NORTH
                        ♠ J 7 6 4
                        ♡ A J
                        ♢ K 10 3
                        ♣ A K J 2
    WEST                               EAST
    ♢ Q 5 2                            ♠ 8 3
    ♡ Q 6 5                            ♡ 8 7 4 3 2
    ♢ Q 5 2                            ♢ 9 8 7 6 4
    ♣ 9 8 7 3                          ♣ 6
                        SOUTH (D)
                        ♠ A K 10 9
                        ♡ K 10 9
                        ♢ A J
                        ♣ Q 10 5 4
```

Both sides were vulnerable.
The bidding:

SOUTH	WEST	NORTH	EAST
1 NT	Pass	6 NT	Dbl.
Pass	Pass		

West led the club nine.

he had second thoughts: East had begun with a singleton club and had doubled, so it was quite likely that he had begun with Q x x x in spades.

Furthermore, if West had begun with a doubleton spade queen, he would be endplayed. So South took the second-round spade finesse and lost to the queen. Unfortunately for him, West still had a spade as a safe lead.

Now it was a matter of guessing one of the red queens, and naturally South, remembering the double and what he knew of the distribution, guessed wrong. He played Crane for the heart queen, and the slam went down.

The kibitzer marveled silently, but North had something to say. "I nearly called the tournament director," he told his partner, "to ask if dummy's rights included the right to repeat the earlier conversation. But I did not think he would know."

JANUARY 5, 1975

OMAR, THE SLAM MAKER

Most players have to learn the hard way that it does not pay to double the opponents in games or slams that they expect to make. But few find the lesson so expensive, or have such a celebrated teacher, as East did on the diagramed deal. It was played in a high-stake rubber bridge game in Paris, and South was Omar Sharif, whose stature in the world of bridge falls only just short of his stature on the movie screens of the world.

West held a freak distribution that occurs about once in a hundred thousand deals. Not unnaturally, he opened four spades, hoping to shut his opponents out of the auction. But North was not willing to be shut out and ventured four notrump. This is generally used to indicate a strong three-suited hand with at most a singleton spade.

When East passed, Sharif jumped confidently to six hearts. He may have been concerned about the possibility of missing a grand slam, but the level was too high for exploration.

East gave way to temptation and doubled. With a likely trump trick, 13 points in high cards, and a singleton in his partner's suit, he no doubt thought he would defeat the slam by at least two tricks. Events showed that he was wrong.

West led the spade ace, which turned out to be a disastrous choice. South ruffed in dummy and noted with pleasure the appearance of the king from East.

Sharif then asked himself why East would double six, lacking any first-round control. The only plausible explanation was that East expected to make a trump trick. So Sharif led the heart seven from dummy and finessed when East played low. When West discarded a spade, East began to feel acutely guilty about his penalty double. But he comforted himself with the thought that he still had potential tricks in the minor suits, and that South could not afford to ruff a second spade in the dummy without suffering an overruff.

The declarer could count eleven sure tricks at this point— seven trumps in his hand, one ruff in dummy, and a trick in each side suit. Another spade ruff was ruled out, for East's spade king was surely a singleton, but there was a good chance of making an extra diamond trick.

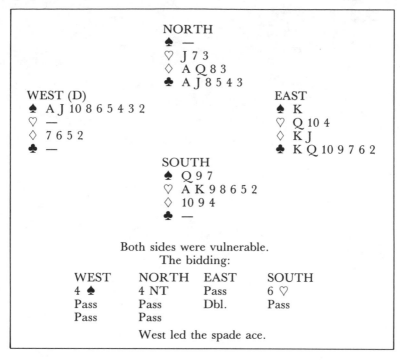

NORTH
♠ —
♡ J 7 3
◇ A Q 8 3
♣ A J 8 5 4 3

WEST (D)
♠ A J 10 8 6 5 4 3 2
♡ —
◇ 7 6 5 2
♣ —

EAST
♠ K
♡ Q 10 4
◇ K J
♣ K Q 10 9 7 6 2

SOUTH
♠ Q 9 7
♡ A K 9 8 6 5 2
◇ 10 9 4
♣ —

Both sides were vulnerable.
The bidding:

WEST	NORTH	EAST	SOUTH
4 ♠	4 NT	Pass	6 ♡
Pass	Pass	Dbl.	Pass
Pass	Pass		

West led the spade ace.

Trumps were drawn, and the diamond ten was finessed, losing to the jack. East returned the club king, and after South discarded the diamond nine—an unblocking play to allow for a possible finesse—South was further astonished and pleased to see West discard a spade. After a little thought, Sharif faced his cards on the table and claimed the remaining tricks, to the stupefaction of East, who demanded an explanation.

"I shall ruff a club and play all my remaining trumps, saving three diamonds in dummy," was the answer. "I know there were nine spades and two void suits on my left, leaving four diamonds originally. West will have to keep two spades, because my nine is a potential trick. So the diamond king is bound to fall when I lead to the ace at the eleventh trick."

The defenders could find no flaw in this dramatic claim by a dramatic star, but they had something to say to each other.

"If you lead anything else," pointed out East, "we would probably beat the slam."

"And if you don't make that greedy double," retorted West, "he would surely have gone down whatever I led."

March 14, 1971

UNUSUAL CIRCUMSTANCES

S omething odd is happening in all the deals in this section. The first concerns the perpetration of a "joke." The second introduced a new dimension to the game when two players were fighting down to the wire for the Mc-Kenney Trophy. The third and fourth have unusual settings: a train and a university common room. And the last is outside the norms of time and space.

STACKING THE DECK

Practical jokers sometimes indulge themselves by stacking a bridge hand for unwary friends. To give each player a complete suit may secure a newspaper mention—and does so about once a year—but is a little too obvious. Equally hackneyed for this purpose are the Duke of Cumberland's hand and the Mississippi Heart hand.

Almost as devastating for the opponents but less well known is the deal shown in the diagram. North–South hope to arrive in seven hearts doubled and might do so by the bidding shown in the diagram if West chooses to open his freak hand with four spades. A greedy redouble is not recommended because West might spoil the fun by escaping into seven spades.

Against seven hearts doubled East counts his chickens but turns out to have a hatching problem. The spade king is led—no other lead would work better—and South wins in the dummy.

At the second trick the queen of diamonds is led, pinning West's jack. East might as well cover with the king, and after winning with the ace South crosses to dummy with a club lead to the ace. The diamond seven is led for a finesse against the nine; and the declarer continues diamonds. On the fourth round dummy's spade loser is discarded, leaving this position:

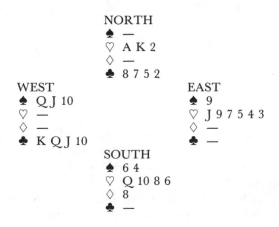

```
                    NORTH
                    ♠ —
                    ♡ A K 2
                    ◇ —
                    ♣ 8 7 5 2
      WEST                          EAST
      ♠ Q J 10                      ♠ 9
      ♡ —                           ♡ J 9 7 5 4 3
      ◇ —                           ◇ —
      ♣ K Q J 10                    ♣ —
                    SOUTH
                    ♠ 6 4
                    ♡ Q 10 8 6
                    ◇ 8
                    ♣ —
```

The declarer ruffs a spade with dummy's deuce of hearts and

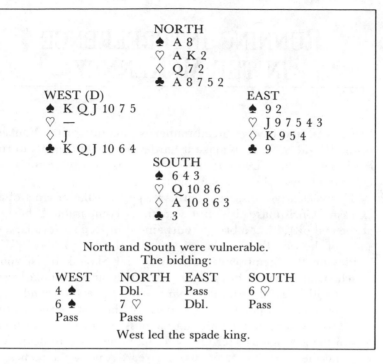

NORTH
♠ A 8
♡ A K 2
◇ Q 7 2
♣ A 8 7 5 2

WEST (D)
♠ K Q J 10 7 5
♡ —
◇ J
♣ K Q J 10 6 4

EAST
♠ 9 2
♡ J 9 7 5 4 3
◇ K 9 5 4
♣ 9

SOUTH
♠ 6 4 3
♡ Q 10 8 6
◇ A 10 8 6 3
♣ 3

North and South were vulnerable.
The bidding:

WEST	NORTH	EAST	SOUTH
4 ♠	Dbl.	Pass	6 ♡
6 ♠	7 ♡	Dbl.	Pass
Pass	Pass		

West led the spade king.

cross-ruffs the last six tricks while East underruffs in a very bad temper.

The contract is made, and when North–South admit to a little joke, a dangerous explosion can be expected from the East seat.

JANUARY 5, 1966

RUNNING INTERFERENCE IN THE MCKENNEY

It is 3 A.M. and George Steinbrenner is pitching for the Yankees in the World Series. To make it harder for his opponents to run the bases, he has hired two more top teams to play on the same field simultaneously, at right angles.

This is clearly a bizarre nightmare, perhaps the product of an excess of Christmas spirit. But something comparable happened at the end of 1981 at a bridge tournament in Reno, Nevada, and some of the world's best players were involved.

Playing the Steinbrenner role was Mel Skolnik of Newport Beach, California, a thirty-eight-year-old financier similarly endowed with great determination and a willingness to spend large sums of money in pursuit of his goals. At the first tournament of 1981, soon after attaining life-master rank, he made up his mind to win the prestigious McKenney Trophy, awarded to the player winning the most master points in a year. Among the names on the trophy are some of the greatest figures in the game: Charles Goren, Helen Sobel, Oswald Jacoby, Tobias Stone, Norman Kay, and Edgar Kaplan.

Skolnik planned a Napoleonic campaign with Ron Andersen and Paul Soloway, both previous McKenney winners, as his chiefs of staff. Among his junior officers, seeing action in selected battles, were Mark Lair, Eddie Wold, Ron Smith, Bobby Levin, Peter Weichsel, Garey Hayden, and Gaylor Kasle—enough talent for two World Championship–winning teams.

All went well for six months, and Skolnik led in the race. But then Barry Crane, the match-point wizard from Hollywood who had the world's highest collection of master points, made a strong bid to win his fifth McKenney title, though trailing by 356 points. When the year's final tournament began in Reno on December 26, he trailed Skolnik by 125 points, a margin that was likely—but not certain—to be decisive.

Crane scored heavily by winning two pairs events and placing second in another, but Skolnik stayed ahead by winning the knockout teams. His lead was 41 points at the start of the concluding event, the Swiss Teams. Three hours from the end of the

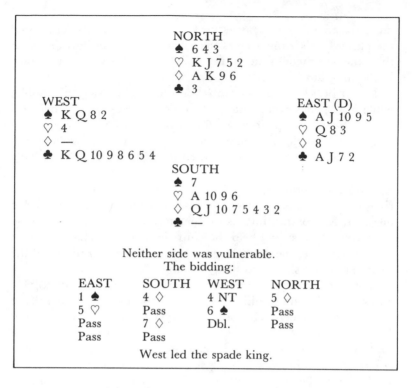

NORTH
♠ 6 4 3
♡ K J 7 5 2
◇ A K 9 6
♣ 3

WEST
♠ K Q 8 2
♡ 4
◇ —
♣ K Q 10 9 8 6 5 4

EAST (D)
♠ A J 10 9 5
♡ Q 8 3
◇ 8
♣ A J 7 2

SOUTH
♠ 7
♡ A 10 9 6
◇ Q J 10 7 5 4 3 2
♣ —

Neither side was vulnerable.
The bidding:

EAST	SOUTH	WEST	NORTH
1 ♠	4 ◇	4 NT	5 ◇
5 ♡	Pass	6 ♠	Pass
Pass	7 ◇	Dbl.	Pass
Pass	Pass		

West led the spade king.

tournament and four from the end of the year, Crane still had a chance, but he could not quite manage the victory that would have snatched the McKenney Trophy from Skolnik.

In the scramble for points, both players were competing in every possible event, sometimes beginning play at 8:45 A.M. and ending at 3 A.M. Some unusual strategies were developed for the occasion. While Skolnik competed in the nonsmoking division of a pairs championship, some of his troops were assigned to the smoking division in an attempt, vain as it turned out, to prevent a Crane victory.

A more unusual case of running interference occurred in a speedball Swiss Teams beginning at midnight. This event would usually be spurned by the experts, but 12 master points would go to the winners and every point seemed vital. So the Skolnik army entered two teams, as did Crane, in the hope of making life harder for the opposition. This was a strange situation without parallel and suggests the Steinbrenner nightmare with which this piece began.

In the final match of this event, one Skolnik regiment met

another, creating a tricky ethical situation. Officials monitored the play to satisfy themselves that everyone was performing with the expected vigor. One strange deal from this match is shown in the diagram.

It can be seen that six clubs for East–West was unbeatable, while six spades would have required double-dummy defense. After a highly competitive auction. Soloway as South had to decide whether to defend against that contract. East's five-heart bid conventionally showed two aces, so the chances of defense were not good.

After long thought, Soloway bid seven diamonds, which was right in practice. Against six spades, he would not have underled his heart ace, permitting his partner to return the club singleton for a ruff. If West had held the club ace, he might have led that card, permitting the doubled grand slam to make. But he led the spade king and shifted to the club king.

It was necessary to guess the hearts, and South did so. He announced that he would draw trumps and eventually play East for the heart queen. He judged that West would not have bid Blackwood with two quick heart losers. In the replay, the same contract went down two, so Soloway gained 5 international match points. And as he was playing for the Skolnik second regiment at the time, he gained them against his commanding officer, though losing the match.

January 10, 1982

HOW AN EXPERT WENT AND LOST IT IN THE COMMON ROOM

Leading somebody astray is usually thought a deplorable proceeding. At the bridge table the victim is almost always one's partner, who becomes understandably abusive when the hand is over. In some rare cases an opponent may become the victim by being diverted from a line of play that would succeed and induced to undertake one that fails.

One of the most diverting diversions of this kind on record resulted in a swing of record proportions. It was allegedly played in a low-stake rubber bridge game and was most entertainingly described in *The Ontario Kibitzer* by life master Dave Silver of London, Ontario, who was inveigled into a common-room game at an institution of learning. His ego inflated with the legitimate pride of a life master sitting down with players without established tournament records, he found himself with a Japanese exchange student as his partner, a poet on his left, and an attractive young lady on his right.

Silver reports that he was slightly deflated by some early misfortunes when the diagramed deal came along. For reasons that must remain a mystery, both East and West chose not to bid their long suits, and North–South had the bidding to themselves.

Silver, sitting South, made an unusual rebid after he had opened one diamond and his partner had responded one spade. A player with a strong balanced hand can normally open two notrump, or jump to two notrump at his second turn after two suits have been bid.

Most experts therefore reserve the double-jump rebid to three notrump for a rare tactical situation. The opener must have a long solid minor suit with stoppers in the unbid suits. South's hand fitted this pattern up to a point, but his diamond suit was not as solid as it might have been.

The partner of the three notrump bidder must be very cautious about persevering in his own suit, for the opener may well have a singleton. Nevertheless, North was somewhat too cautious in this case. He could have made four spades, and the disaster that developed would have been averted.

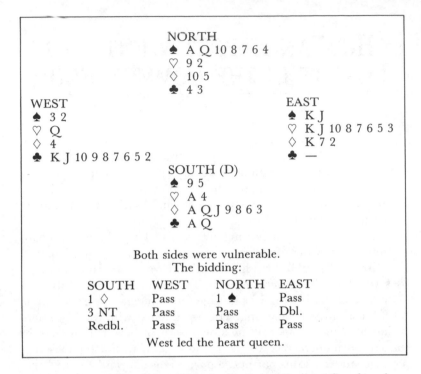

NORTH
♠ A Q 10 8 7 6 4
♡ 9 2
◇ 10 5
♣ 4 3

WEST
♠ 3 2
♡ Q
◇ 4
♣ K J 10 9 8 7 6 5 2

EAST
♠ K J
♡ K J 10 8 7 6 5 3
◇ K 7 2
♣ —

SOUTH (D)
♠ 9 5
♡ A 4
◇ A Q J 9 8 6 3
♣ A Q

Both sides were vulnerable.
The bidding:

SOUTH	WEST	NORTH	EAST
1 ◇	Pass	1 ♠	Pass
3 NT	Pass	Pass	Dbl.
Redbl.	Pass	Pass	Pass

West led the heart queen.

The young lady sitting East doubled timidly, and South redoubled in ringing masculine tones. This discouraged North from any thoughts he may have had of retreating to four spades at this point. The redouble surely indicated that South held nine sure tricks in his hand, and that the doubler was out of line.

If West had led a club three redoubled overtricks for a score of 2,150 would have been conceivable. When West led his singleton heart queen, having worked out that his partner must have great length in that suit, the declarer was still apparently headed for ten tricks.

South's main chance was to find the diamond king on his right, guarded not more than twice. And he could see an extra chance if East held a singleton spade king. Accordingly, he won the opening lead in his hand with the heart ace, after East had played the king, and led to the spade ace.

Perhaps East was expecting the queen of spades to be finessed. In any event, by accident or genius, she dropped the spade king, a brilliant diversionary move.

South now thought that he knew the spade situation. Pausing only to offer "a friendly admonition about the futility of making speculative doubles of famous life masters," he led to his diamond ace and confidently finessed the spade ten. This lost to the jack, and East produced a deluge of hearts. South would have made one more trick at the end if he had saved the queen–jack of diamonds. But he not unnaturally clung to his ace–queen of clubs, and East made the last two tricks with the king and seven of diamonds.

"There was a break in the action," reports Silver, "as we enlisted the services of a Ph.D. from the mathematics department to help calculate the penalty. My Japanese partner, who had become increasingly scrutable as the hand had progressed, or rather disintegrated, leaned across the table towards me.

" 'I'm sorry about Pearl Harbor,' he whispered. 'Are we even now?' "

AUGUST 8, 1971

TRACKING A "TUNNEL BID"

Those accustomed to the competitiveness of tournament play, to the orderly progress of a club game, or to leisurely and sociable home bridge find themselves in a different world if they venture into a railroad commuter game.

A square of green baize is never available, and most players are content with a playing surface consisting of a newspaper or a raincoat. But for most regular groups in the metropolitan New York area, matters are better organized. The conductor provides a board to play on, a deck of cards, and some paper for scoring. For this useful service, he charges each player 25 cents.

The games are nearly always "ghoulies," a procedure that makes for speed and excitement at the cost of horrifying the purist. The cards are not shuffled and are usually dealt seven and six at a time, increasing the chance of freak distributions and repealing the laws of probability in respect to suit divisions.

The stakes are usually a tenth or a fifth of a cent, leading to a hurried transfer of small coins when the train pulls to a halt. But in Long Island games there is sometimes a bonus for the winning partnership, a circumstance that may give rise to a "tunnel bid." This is a wild effort to turn defeat into victory in the last ninety seconds as the train grinds to a halt in Penn Station.

"The greatest perversion of the game of bridge" is how the tunnel bid is described by Charles Howard of Great Neck, New York, one of the sharpest octogenarian players one could find anywhere. He produced one himself on the diagramed deal by opening four clubs as South.

North took a quick look out of the window and raised to six clubs, a reasonable shot in the circumstances. And when this was indignantly doubled by East, he redoubled loudly.

With a neutral lead, South would have been able to ruff a diamond in the dummy and make his contract easily. But West, who was regretting the customary tardiness of the train that had made this deal possible, pulled himself together and found the most effective lead of a trump.

East took the ace, returned a trump to dummy's king, and sat back happily to wait for another trick or two. South now had a choice of plans. In a world championship it would no doubt be

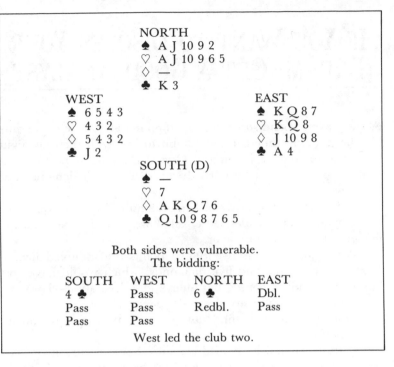

NORTH
♠ A J 10 9 2
♡ A J 10 9 6 5
◇ —
♣ K 3

WEST
♠ 6 5 4 3
♡ 4 3 2
◇ 5 4 3 2
♣ J 2

EAST
♠ K Q 8 7
♡ K Q 8
◇ J 10 9 8
♣ A 4

SOUTH (D)
♠ —
♡ 7
◇ A K Q 7 6
♣ Q 10 9 8 7 6 5

Both sides were vulnerable.
The bidding:

SOUTH	WEST	NORTH	EAST
4 ♣	Pass	6 ♣	Dbl.
Pass	Pass	Redbl.	Pass
Pass	Pass		

West led the club two.

right to cash the spade ace, ruff a spade, and lead all the remaining trumps from the closed hand. With the actual lie of the cards, this brings about a squeeze in the red suits and East is helpless.

But this squeeze is a long shot. It works only if East has not only the king–queen of hearts, quite likely in the light of his double, but also the only protection in diamonds. That means he must have five or more diamonds, or exactly J 10 9 8.

Howard adopted a different line of play, which could not succeed against the best defense but had excellent prospects in the tunnel. He cashed the heart, ruffed a heart, and ran all his trumps. He had thus stranded the spade ace in the dummy, but East did not know it. On the last trump, East had to choose whether to throw a spade from king–queen or a diamond from J 10 9 8.

In more peaceful circumstances the defense could solve the problem. West could throw away all his diamonds or all his spades, and East would know what to do. But in the tunnel it was not easy. East parted with a diamond, and Howard scored five diamond tricks to make his redoubled slam.

August 17, 1980

IF YOU WANT TO DISCUSS YOUR DREAM, GET A GOOD ANALYST

A few players spend so much time thinking about the game during the day that they carry the habit to bed with them at night and dream about bridge hands. One of my regular partners recently reported the diagramed dream deal, which demonstrates ace power.

"I often take chances when I'm dreaming," South explained, "so I opened four spades. After all, I was in third bed and the vulnerability was in my favor.

"West looked at his twenty-two points and doubled firmly. East thought of bidding five diamonds, which would have cost him eight hundred points, but after a long hesitation—I was almost going to sleep in my sleep—he passed."

"You were lucky to find dummy with two trumps and an ace," I observed.

"Fortune favors the bold dreamer," South went on. "They could not beat me. After the lead of the heart king, I simply maneuvered to ruff two diamonds."

On awakening, my partner had scribbled the deal on a piece of paper. I glanced at it and made a hasty comment.

"It would not be true to say that they could not beat you with any lead," I pointed out. "If West had dropped the spade king on the table, and such things happen, especially late at night, your dream would have become a nightmare. If you then ruff one diamond in the dummy, he gets his trump trick back."

"Not at all," the dreaming declarer retorted. "I play for the clubs to be three–three. I take the spade ace and play the club ace and a club. Then they cannot prevent me from establishing clubs and discarding one diamond loser on the fourth round of clubs to make the game."

"As I've always suspected, your analysis when you're awake is worse than mine when I'm asleep," my wife concluded smugly.

FEBRUARY 9, 1974

NORTH (D)
♠ Q 4
♡ 9 7 6 4 3
◇ A
♣ 8 7 4 3 2

WEST
♠ K J 9
♡ K Q J 2
◇ K Q J
♣ K Q J

EAST
♠ 10
♡ 10 8 5
◇ 10 9 8 5 4 2
♣ 10 9 5

SOUTH
♠ A 8 7 6 5 3 2
♡ A
◇ 7 6 3
♣ A 6

East and West were vulnerable.
The bidding:

NORTH	EAST	SOUTH	WEST
Pass	Pass	4 ♠	Dbl.
Pass	Pass	Pass	

West led the heart king.

FICTION

On the first two deals in this section someone takes you by the arm and tests your credulity. The next two feature imaginative efforts by two notable bridge writers. And finally an anonymous reader focuses on an unusual date.

BRIDGE, BROOKLYN

Most tournament players are accustomed to being approached by some total stranger and asked to listen to a hand. Sometimes the stranger genuinely wants advice on how he should have bid or played. More often, he wants to unburden a sad story or get support for his opinion that his partner was to blame for a disaster. And occasionally he is a con man, claiming credit for a winning line of play discovered in subsequent cerebration. He may even offer a famous coup or a double-dummy problem, the equivalent of selling the Brooklyn Bridge.

With these warnings in mind, consider how you would judge the following episode. A smooth-spoken stranger approaches you and thrusts a piece of paper under your nose, on which are the West and North hands shown in the diagram.

"I was West," explains the S.S.S., "and there was a one-spade opening on my right. I might have bid one notrump, but I doubled and North raised the spades. When this came round to me, I doubled again. Got that?"

"Yes," you admit reluctantly, looking for means of escape. But he has you firmly by the arm. "Believe it or not," he goes on, "my partner passed my second takeout double. He's crazy. All my partners are crazy."

You mutter something to the effect that most people get the partners they deserve, but he is not listening.

"I led the club ace," he continues, "and my partner played the deuce. Now I had to try to beat this silly contract. What would you have done?"

"I have no idea," you admit, avoiding mental effort without straining the truth.

"I led the heart king," he announces unblushingly, "and that was the only way to beat the contract. Here, look at the other hands."

You look in astonishment.

"South won the heart ace and led a trump. I put up the spade ace and gave my partner a heart ruff. He shifted to the diamond queen, assuring us two diamond tricks and another heart ruff for one down. Any other play at trick two and they would have made it."

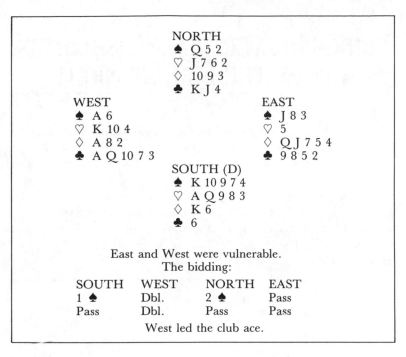

NORTH
♠ Q 5 2
♡ J 7 6 2
◇ 10 9 3
♣ K J 4

WEST
♠ A 6
♡ K 10 4
◇ A 8 2
♣ A Q 10 7 3

EAST
♠ J 8 3
♡ 5
◇ Q J 7 5 4
♣ 9 8 5 2

SOUTH (D)
♠ K 10 9 7 4
♡ A Q 9 8 3
◇ K 6
♣ 6

East and West were vulnerable.
The bidding:

SOUTH	WEST	NORTH	EAST
1 ♠	Dbl.	2 ♠	Pass
Pass	Dbl.	Pass	Pass

West led the club ace.

"Well played," you say with well-feigned enthusiasm. "I hope your partner congratulated you."

"He did not. He just told me I could have beaten it more easily by leading a heart at trick one."

You escape and review his story. If you believe it, I'd be happy to meet you. I could perhaps sell you a bridge, quite cheaply.

DECEMBER 16, 1973

BRIDGE PLAYERS, LIKE FISHERMEN, LIE BY THE FIRE AT NIGHT

Fishermen boast about the one that got away without considering that failure might be regarded as a reflection on their skill. Bridge players, however, are more sensitive and find different ways to distort the truth.

If they let a very big one get away, they do not make it even bigger so their failure will be more understandable. Instead, they imply that somebody else let it get away, or even contend that they caught it. They do not, after all, have to produce a corpus for the kitchen scale.

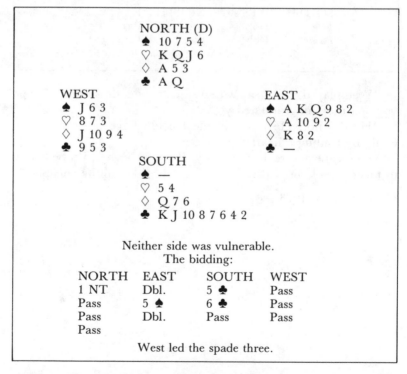

```
                    NORTH (D)
                    ♠ 10 7 5 4
                    ♡ K Q J 6
                    ◊ A 5 3
                    ♣ A Q
      WEST                            EAST
      ♠ J 6 3                         ♠ A K Q 9 8 2
      ♡ 8 7 3                         ♡ A 10 9 2
      ◊ J 10 9 4                      ◊ K 8 2
      ♣ 9 5 3                         ♣ —
                    SOUTH
                    ♠ —
                    ♡ 5 4
                    ◊ Q 7 6
                    ♣ K J 10 8 7 6 4 2
```

Neither side was vulnerable.
The bidding:

NORTH	EAST	SOUTH	WEST
1 NT	Dbl.	5 ♣	Pass
Pass	5 ♠	6 ♣	Pass
Pass	Dbl.	Pass	Pass
Pass			

West led the spade three.

The unknown declarer who missed the opportunity of a life-time on the diagramed deal is probably now asserting that he made the contract—or at least that somebody else went down. It was played in a rubber bridge game in a London club, and South held a freak collection. When his partner opened one notrump and East doubled, he naturally jumped to five clubs. He had a harder decision on the next round when East bid his suit.

Five spades would have failed by two tricks, but South was in no mood to defend. He pushed on to six clubs and was duly doubled by East. A spade was led, and South eventually lost a trick in each red suit for down one.

In the postmortem it was pointed out to him that he had missed the opportunity of a bridge lifetime. The right play after ruffing the first trick was to enter dummy twice in trumps to ruff two more spades. This would leave East with the only spade protection. One more round of trumps would leave this position:

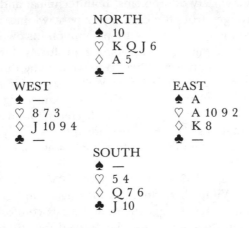

On the next trump lead a diamond would be thrown from dummy and East would be finished. If he threw a heart or a spade, South would lead a heart with decisive effect. And if he threw a diamond, South would lead that suit, return to his hand with a spade ruff, and cash the diamond queen. Then a heart lead would score two heart tricks in dummy.

If South had done this, he would have won lasting fame as the man who made a doubled slam with a triple trump squeeze without the count. And East would have been left screaming at his partner for his failure to lead a diamond.

FEBRUARY 21, 1983

IT IS BETTER
TO BE SMUG THAN UNLUCKY

The psychology of lesser players is a fascinating study largely ignored by bridge writers. The supreme authority in this area was Skid Simon, an Englishman of Russian origin who was not only a master player but a master writer who produced a series of entertaining novels.

In his classic *Why You Lose at Bridge,* Simon introduced four players with a variety of problems, both technical and psychological. These ranged from the Unlucky Expert, who assumes, quite wrongly, that the other players are playing on his own high level, to Mrs. Guggenheim, who apologizes profusely for her many errors and whose partners all try to make her the dummy.

The other characters are Futile Willie, who has read all the books but lacks judgment in applying his knowledge, and Mr. Smug, whose common sense and luck count for more than his technical limitations. Some of the adventures of this foursome were described by Simon in his last book, long out of print, entitled *Cut for Partners.*

In the diagramed deal the Unlucky Expert sits South partnering Futile Willie. Mr. Smug is looking complacently at the West hand, and Mrs. Guggenheim as East is comforting herself with the thought that she cannot be blamed for anything on this hand.

In his comments on the bidding, Simon gave South a good mark for his six-heart bid:

"His partner's raise to five followed by the refusal to double five spades could only be construed as an invitation to bid six. As he held both minor aces, this invitation could only be based on very strong heart support and a spade void, or a singleton spade and one or both of the minor kings.

"This is a nice example of a series of inferences by which a quite exciting hand, viewed solo, becomes a very good hand indeed when viewed alongside the bidding. Place your hand alongside of what is known of your partner's on the bidding and start playing it mentally. You should soon reach a stage when you can look sadly at an ace and wish it had a different color. But don't

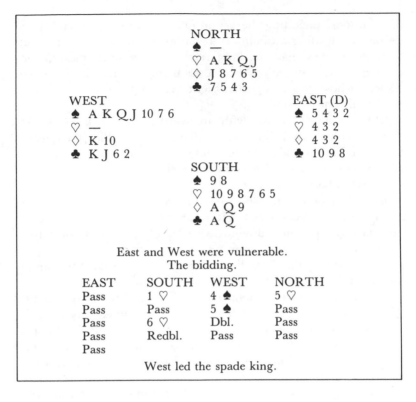

NORTH
♠ —
♡ A K Q J
◇ J 8 7 6 5
♣ 7 5 4 3

WEST
♠ A K Q J 10 7 6
♡ —
◇ K 10
♣ K J 6 2

EAST (D)
♠ 5 4 3 2
♡ 4 3 2
◇ 4 3 2
♣ 10 9 8

SOUTH
♠ 9 8
♡ 10 9 8 7 6 5
◇ A Q 9
♣ A Q

East and West were vulnerable.
The bidding.

EAST	SOUTH	WEST	NORTH
Pass	1 ♡	4 ♠	5 ♡
Pass	Pass	5 ♠	Pass
Pass	6 ♡	Dbl.	Pass
Pass	Redbl.	Pass	Pass
Pass			

West led the spade king.

consider you have arrived until you can look at a solitary queen and love it.''

Mr. Smug made a typically greedy double of six hearts, expecting a two- or three-trick defeat. He expected to make a spade trick, at least one of his kings, and perhaps a trump trick in his partner's hand.

''The Unlucky Expert showed his delight at the double (which means that one corner of his mouth twitched slightly), for what could West be doubling on except K x of trumps, which he imagined were on the right side? But he hesitated a little before redoubling. Would Mr. Smug go six spades?

''Tcha, thought Mr. Smug, you can't bluff me.''

The opening spade lead was ruffed, and Mr. Smug felt wounded. South drew a round of trumps, discovered the break, and settled down to work it out. He was inclined to think that West had eight spades to justify his bidding, and there was a distinct possibility of a singleton diamond.

So South worked out a plan that would succeed against several distributions, including the actual one. There was something to be said for leading a diamond to the nine, but he chose to lead to the ace. West had the king ready, expecting a finesse, and dropped it. He concealed his distress manfully, and the Unlucky Expert, whose psychological insight falls well short of his technical skill, noticed nothing.

"Six hearts redoubled with an overtrick, he thought. Enter dummy with a trump. Finesse the diamond nine. Play the queen, to which East would have to follow, and enter dummy with a trump. Throw the two losers on the established diamonds. Bridge isn't such a bad game after all."

But when South finessed the diamond nine, Mr. Smug dramatically produced the ten. He returned a spade, forcing dummy's last trump. The diamonds were left blocked, and South had no way to escape a club loser.

"Of course I didn't pull the wrong card," said Mr. Smug indignantly. "I saw what was coming."

"I was terribly frightened, partner," said Mrs. Guggenheim. "I had such a bad hand I felt sure they could make anything."

Simon's verdict, a little harsh, was that the Unlucky Expert had given away 1,920 points by failing to make a simple slam. When the diamond king fell, he could have continued with the queen to make six in safety.

"Once again," said the narrator, "Mr. Smug can't be charged anything for his various atrocities on the hand. The luck of the man!"

June 24, 1973

SUICIDAL KINGS
ARE DANGEROUS TO DOCTORS

The ability to look more than one trick into the future is one of the hallmarks of the expert, and nowhere is it more dramatically demonstrated than in a sacrifice play. An entertaining article on this theme by Ernst Theimer of Rumson, New Jersey, appeared in the December 1968 issue of *The Bridge World*. The setting is a rehabilitation institute, and the central character is a minor monarch who developed suicidal tendencies after being deposed by revolutionaries. This mental condition was improved when he took up bridge, but he developed an overpowering urge to hurl kings to their destruction.

Not only did he destroy his own kings, but he also destroyed the opposing declarers. Every now and again, he would turn red in the face, sneeze, hiccup, and make the sacrificial play needed to defeat the contract. On the diagramed deal he had occasion to hiccup three times in one hand.

The king sat West and doubled the opening bid of one spade. North, a poor player, bid two diamonds when he should have bid two spades, and his side reached four spades. East tried a sacrifice in five clubs, which would have been down two, and South, an expert, persevered to five spades. He was annoyed by the opposing sacrifice bid and was even more annoyed by the subsequent sacrifices in the play.

The king turned red, sneezed, hiccupped, and pushed out the diamond king as the opening lead. This rather improbable move gave away a sure trick, but was the defense's only chance to beat the contract.

With the normal lead of the club king, South would have had no trouble in making his contract. He would have won with the ace and led the spade queen, after which he could not have been prevented from making use of dummy's diamonds. If West ducked, the trumps would be cleared, and the diamond king would later be allowed to capture the queen and win a trick. Or if West won the first trump lead and shifted brilliantly to the diamond king, South would be able to take two diamond tricks

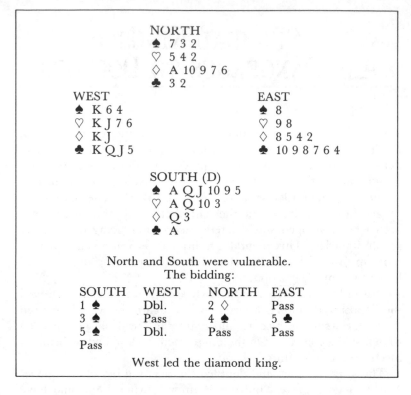

NORTH
♠ 7 3 2
♡ 5 4 2
◇ A 10 9 7 6
♣ 3 2

WEST
♠ K 6 4
♡ K J 7 6
◇ K J
♣ K Q J 5

EAST
♠ 8
♡ 9 8
◇ 8 5 4 2
♣ 10 9 8 7 6 4

SOUTH (D)
♠ A Q J 10 9 5
♡ A Q 10 3
◇ Q 3
♣ A

North and South were vulnerable.
The bidding:

SOUTH	WEST	NORTH	EAST
1 ♠	Dbl.	2 ◇	Pass
3 ♠	Pass	4 ♠	5 ♣
5 ♠	Dbl.	Pass	Pass
Pass			

West led the diamond king.

and draw trumps ending in dummy, making an overtrick.

West's hara-kiri with the diamond king slaughtered South when properly followed up. The declarer won with the ace in dummy and led to his diamond queen, collecting the jack. There was a chance of using the diamonds if the spade seven became an entry to the dummy.

South therefore led the spade queen, and West sneezed and played low. The jack was continued, and West hiccupped loudly and played low again. Both these ducking plays were necessary to prevent South from reaching the dummy with the spade seven to cash the diamonds.

The spade king was now dead, and South gathered it in with his ace, but so was the dummy. The declarer cashed his remaining three trumps, giving West a discarding problem. With great foresight, he threw one heart and the queen–jack of clubs, leaving this position:

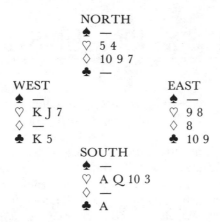

NORTH
♠ —
♡ 5 4
◊ 10 9 7
♣ —

WEST
♠ —
♡ K J 7
◊ —
♣ K 5

EAST
♠ —
♡ 9 8
◊ 8
♣ 10 9

SOUTH
♠ —
♡ A Q 10 3
◊ —
♣ A

When South led the club ace, West gave a final hiccup and dropped the club king. This irritated South, who led the heart queen in the hope of a fourth king sacrifice. But West had run out of sneezes and hiccups. He won with the heart king and led the club five, enabling East to lead his last heart and defeat the contract.

The doctors in the institute insisted on playing for purely nominal stakes, ostensibly to avoid taking advantage of their royal patient's mental instability. But it seems more likely that they were afraid of losing their stethoscopes.

JANUARY 12, 1969

SIX, SIX, PICK UP STICKS

Almost all rules have to be broken eventually, and this applies to bridge writers as well as players. I do not normally quote verbatim from material submitted by readers, nor publish freak deals, nor pay any attention to correspondents using fictitious names and addresses. The following, however, represents an exception to all three rules. It is a letter headed 666 East 66th Street, New York, 66, and it is signed "Looey the Rat."

"It gives me great pleasure to announce the Centennial Sickly Six Bridge Tournament, which will take place June 6, 1966 (6/6/66). Since this date occurs only once a century, our last tournament was held in 1866. This year's tournament will take place 7:06 P.M. (6:66) at 666 East 66th Street and will have loco rating.

"Here is an interesting hand which arose in the 1866 tournament:

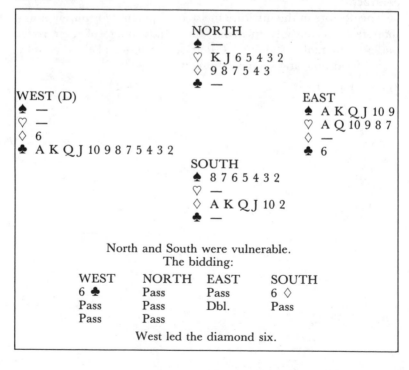

```
                        NORTH
                        ♠ —
                        ♡ K J 6 5 4 3 2
                        ◊ 9 8 7 5 4 3
                        ♣ —
WEST (D)                                        EAST
♠ —                                             ♠ A K Q J 10 9
♡ —                                             ♡ A Q 10 9 8 7
◊ 6                                             ◊ —
♣ A K Q J 10 9 8 7 5 4 3 2                      ♣ 6
                        SOUTH
                        ♠ 8 7 6 5 4 3 2
                        ♡ —
                        ◊ A K Q J 10 2
                        ♣ —
```

North and South were vulnerable.
The bidding:

WEST	NORTH	EAST	SOUTH
6 ♣	Pass	Pass	6 ◊
Pass	Pass	Dbl.	Pass
Pass	Pass		

West led the diamond six.

"East had been playing bridge for 66 years and had entered the tournament because he needed only .06 point in order to become a life master. West and South were charter members of the Six, and North was—well, North was dummy.

"West knew that he had been dealt the six of diamonds for a purpose, so he led it. Indeed, with a club lead, once South found out about the spade situation, he could safely cross-ruff the hand. If East had the six of diamonds, he would not be able to overruff.

"After South played the diamond seven to the first trick, East had to discard the club six. If he discarded a heart, South could eventually establish a heart trick in dummy by ruffing. If he discarded a spade, South could overtake the trump trick in his own hand and eventually establish a spade trick.

"South won the first trick in his hand with the ace, as a sheer display of power, and started cross-ruffing spades and hearts. Short of one trick, South reduced the hand to the following position:

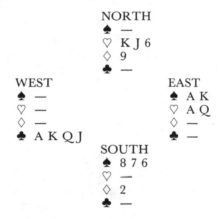

```
                  NORTH
                  ♠ —
                  ♡ K J 6
                  ◇ 9
                  ♣ —
   WEST                        EAST
   ♠ —                         ♠ A K
   ♡ —                         ♡ A Q
   ◇ —                         ◇ —
   ♣ A K Q J                   ♣ —
                  SOUTH
                  ♠ 8 7 6
                  ♡ —
                  ◇ 2
                  ♣ —
```

"South played the six of spades from his hand and West discarded the jack of clubs. Noticing that by trumping he was bound to lose two tricks eventually, South consoled himself by playing a six on a six, letting East win the trick with the spade king. At this point East threw his cards on the table, for he had just been endplayed. If he led the ace of spades, South would trump it in dummy and South's hand would be good. If East led the ace of hearts, South would trump it in his hand and dummy's hand would be good.

122

"Result: South made six diamonds doubled and won ⅔ of a master point, or .66666. . . . East was never seen again and North was unhappy because every six had lost a trick."

10

THE HUMAN FACTOR

B ridge is, so far, played almost entirely by human beings with human frailties. Computers, which are excellent at chess, are rather naïve bridge performers. They should stick to their familiar role of dealing tournament hands, although that can, as discussed in our first sample, arouse misplaced resentment.

We also have the unpleasant self-appointed expert getting his just deserts; the perennial optimist; a quintet of postmortem characters; and a Frenchman killed by kindness.

COMPUTER PARANOIA

Paranoia is a disease of tournament bridge players. They feel themselves to be victims of modern technology—the computer is out to get them. The deals for most forms of tournament play are produced by a computer, which accurately simulates a random shuffle but still gets the blame whenever a freak deal crops up. The complainants fail to appreciate that if the computer did not produce a freak deal now and again it would not be doing its job. The diagramed hand is an example of a rubber bridge freak: West's 9-4-0-0 distribution is something he can expect once in a hundred thousand deals.

East opened light with one spade, and South naturally jumped to four hearts. West had two problems to consider "at this point in time," as they say in Washington, and he confronted only one of them. The first problem, a technical judgment, was what contract could be made with such an incredibly freak collection, and he decided, correctly as it turned out, that six diamonds would be about right.

But this ignored the tactical problem: how to become the declarer. With such distribution, it is vital to play the hand, and the level at which it is played is of lesser importance. The best strategy was to bid five diamonds, a clear underbid, hoping to be pushed to six diamonds and willing to go to seven diamonds if necessary.

As it was, six diamonds pushed North to six hearts. West might have continued to seven diamonds, but was halted by his partner's double, a questionable decision. East no doubt feared that a pass would be construed as an invitation to bid seven diamonds, but with three diamonds in his hand he should have realized that his defensive prospects were uncertain.

A look at the diagram suggests that East–West were right to defend six hearts rather than persevere to seven diamonds and go one down. It seems that South has two unavoidable spade losers, for even if he can establish two club tricks in the dummy, that will allow him only two discards.

But Charles Howard of Great Neck, sitting South, found a road to twelve tricks after West made the normal lead of the diamond ace. The declarer blenched when he saw dummy's three

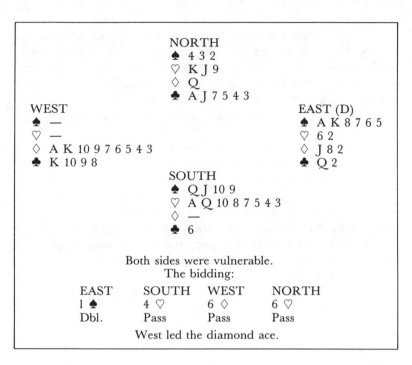

NORTH
♠ 4 3 2
♡ K J 9
◇ Q
♣ A J 7 5 4 3

WEST
♠ —
♡ —
◇ A K 10 9 7 6 5 4 3
♣ K 10 9 8

EAST (D)
♠ A K 8 7 6 5
♡ 6 2
◇ J 8 2
♣ Q 2

SOUTH
♠ Q J 10 9
♡ A Q 10 8 7 5 4 3
◇ —
♣ 6

Both sides were vulnerable.
The bidding:

EAST	SOUTH	WEST	NORTH
1 ♠	4 ♡	6 ◇	6 ♡
Dbl.	Pass	Pass	Pass

West led the diamond ace.

small spades, but at least they had not led the suit—perhaps West was void. There was no choice but to start developing clubs, so after ruffing the first trick South led to the ace and ruffed a club. He entered dummy with a trump lead to the nine and ruffed another club high. Dummy was entered with another trump lead, leaving this position:

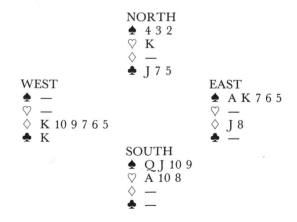

NORTH
♠ 4 3 2
♡ K
◇ —
♣ J 7 5

WEST
♠ —
♡ —
◇ K 10 9 7 6 5
♣ K

EAST
♠ A K 7 6 5
♡ —
◇ J 8
♣ —

SOUTH
♠ Q J 10 9
♡ A 10 8
◇ —
♣ —

West was known to have begun with four clubs and a void in hearts. The bidding and the lack of a spade lead suggested that he held nine diamonds originally and a void in spades. On that analysis there was a solution. The declarer led a club from dummy and discarded a spade. West had to win and concede a ruff and sluff, allowing South to dispose of all his remaining spades to make the doubled slam.

"Beautifully played, partner," announced North enthusiastically. "I felt sure you were going to go down."

"I had the hand of a lifetime," moaned West, "and the opponents make an unbeatable slam against me."

"It was not unbeatable," East told him after some thought. "All you had to do was to lead a club, and the declarer would have been an entry short. He could not have removed dummy's diamond, and you would have had a safe diamond lead later instead of being endplayed."

"Leave me alone," screamed West. "I was paranoid before."

JULY 29, 1973

COMEUPPANCE

Bridge is essentially a social game, but unfortunately it attracts a substantial percentage of antisocial people. The nuisance is prevalent at every level—in major tournaments, in small clubs, and in private homes. The menace is perhaps worst in a domestic game, since there is no escape, short of breaking up the game, from the self-appointed expert who moans about his luck, screams at his partner, jeers at his opponents, and offers them unsolicited advice.

The guilty party quite fails to realize that he is not only spoiling his own interests, but his partner's performance will also deteriorate in such circumstances and so will his own. To illustrate this, consider a case history. The unpleasant Mr. X was sitting West, playing with his wife against Mr. and Mrs. Y, who were North and South, respectively.

East opened one notrump and correctly advised the opponents when her partner made an artificial response of two hearts.

"That is a transfer bid," she volunteered. "Harry has long spades and wants me to play the hand."

"No, I don't," he snapped. "Not after the way you played the last hand. I expect I should have bid three spades just to make you the dummy."

This remark was quite improper, since it implied that he had a game-going hand. Influenced by this, East jumped to three spades instead of making the normal bid of two spades. But all roads would have led to four spades.

"I bid four spades," announced West. "And it's your lead," he added prematurely, turning to South.

"No it's not," retorted Mrs. Y, goaded into highly speculative action. "It's my bid, and I bid five hearts."

"Mabel's lost her marbles," jeered West. "You'll probably go down 1,400 dear, and it'll serve you right."

"It'll be a good save if I go down only two," responded South, with more confidence than she felt.

Still jeering, West led the spade king and proceeded to misdefend. He might have justified his prediction of a 1,400 penalty by shifting to a trump at the second trick, for South could have been prevented from reaching the club ace.

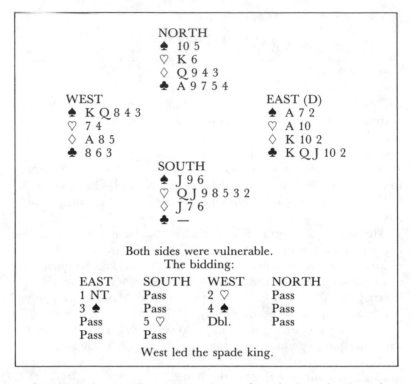

NORTH
♠ 10 5
♡ K 6
◇ Q 9 4 3
♣ A 9 7 5 4

WEST
♠ K Q 8 4 3
♡ 7 4
◇ A 8 5
♣ 8 6 3

EAST (D)
♠ A 7 2
♡ A 10
◇ K 10 2
♣ K Q J 10 2

SOUTH
♠ J 9 6
♡ Q J 9 8 5 3 2
◇ J 7 6
♣ —

Both sides were vulnerable.
The bidding:

EAST	SOUTH	WEST	NORTH
1 NT	Pass	2 ♡	Pass
3 ♠	Pass	4 ♠	Pass
Pass	5 ♡	Dbl.	Pass
Pass	Pass		

West led the spade king.

South made a modest attempt to confuse the issue by dropping the spade jack on the first trick and succeeded unexpectedly well. West felt sure that his partner held four spades and led the spade queen at the second trick. This improved South's prospects, and they improved even further when East overtook the queen with the ace, a play that she was quite unable to justify later to her screaming spouse. The psychological explanation is that she had been demoralized by the verbal harassment she had received earlier in the evening.

At this point, there was no way in which South could be prevented from discarding a diamond on the club ace, and the prospective penalty was down to a mere 800, with two spades, two diamonds, and one heart being the losing tricks. But the Fates, who favor good manners, had another shaft in store for West.

East shifted to the club king, and South threw a diamond loser. The heart ace was forced out, and a club lead was ruffed. After two more heart leads the position was this:

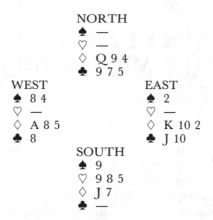

NORTH
♠ —
♡ —
◇ Q 9 4
♣ 9 7 5

WEST
♠ 8 4
♡ —
◇ A 8 5
♣ 8

EAST
♠ 2
♡ —
◇ K 10 2
♣ J 10

SOUTH
♠ 9
♡ 9 8 5
◇ J 7
♣ —

The diamond jack was led, and West made another error by playing low. After East won with the king and South regained the lead by ruffing a club, West imperiously demanded that play cease temporarily while he thought. He laboriously counted the hand. It was clear to him that South had no more black cards, so he must have two more diamonds.

Having worked this out, West smoothly ducked when South led a diamond, thus making his third major error. South put up the queen in dummy, escaping for down two.

Nobody ventured to criticize West, but South was mildly pleased. "It was a good save after all," she ventured.

"I don't go by results," foamed West. "It was a crazy bid." Unlike Voltaire, we may agree with his opinion but deny to the death his right to say it.

APRIL 7, 1974

ENTER OPTIMISTICALLY, DEPART MISTY-OPTICALLY

Pessimists are rarely successful at the bridge table. Their attitude damages their partners' morale and improves their opponents'. If you think the worst will happen, it probably will.

Thus many experts are professional optimists by inclination or calculation, finding silver linings in the darkest clouds. In the wake of any disaster they will find words of cheer for their partners, reminding one of the gentleman who invariably announced, "It might have been worse." When a group of his friends advised him that the previous night Mr. A had found Mr. B with A's wife, shot them both, and then shot himself, he produced his usual, "It might have been worse." "How could it be worse?" "If he'd come on Monday," explained the silver-liner, "he'd have shot me."

An East player belonging to this cheerful coterie fell victim to some fine play by an opposing declarer on the diagramed deal. East's optimism was not to blame for his opening one-spade bid. With two strong five-card major suits almost all experts would do the same. South scraped up an overcall of two diamonds, an action that nearly always requires a six-card suit when vulnerable, and West jumped to three spades. This was a limit raise, suggesting about 10 points in high cards, and a more cautious player would have bid two spades.

North had to make an interesting decision over three spades. He knew his side could do well in diamonds and that the opponents would do well in spades. Whether either side could make a game was not clear. His jump to five diamonds had a triple objective. It would be right if East–West could make four spades; or if North–South could make five diamonds; or if East–West could be pushed to five spades.

Notice that North placed little value on his spade king, since he expected East to hold the spade ace. And South had placed no value at all on his spade queen. Separately they would have been worthless, but in combination they were worth a trick. In the strange mathematics of the card table, it may happen that $0 + 0 = 1$.

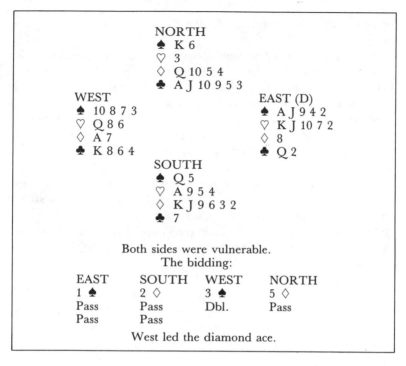

NORTH
- ♠ K 6
- ♡ 3
- ◇ Q 10 5 4
- ♣ A J 10 9 5 3

WEST
- ♠ 10 8 7 3
- ♡ Q 8 6
- ◇ A 7
- ♣ K 8 6 4

EAST (D)
- ♠ A J 9 4 2
- ♡ K J 10 7 2
- ◇ 8
- ♣ Q 2

SOUTH
- ♠ Q 5
- ♡ A 9 5 4
- ◇ K J 9 6 3 2
- ♣ 7

Both sides were vulnerable.
The bidding:

EAST	SOUTH	WEST	NORTH
1 ♠	2 ◇	3 ♠	5 ◇
Pass	Pass	Dbl.	Pass
Pass	Pass		

West led the diamond ace.

East resisted the temptation to carry on to five spades over five diamonds, and West not unnaturally doubled. He had defensive assets, and his partner had opened the bidding. It was likely that North had made an "advance save," expecting to fail in five diamonds, an assessment that was not far from the truth.

West made a good decision in choosing an opening lead. He judged that the declarer would need ruffs and therefore led the ace of diamonds followed by his remaining trump. This made South's task as difficult as possible, but he was equal to the occasion. The declarer was Larry Weiss of Los Angeles, one of the best West Coast players.

South had only two obvious losers, but he was now short of a winner, since the defense had unkindly deprived him of the opportunity of ruffing all his small hearts in the dummy. He set out to establish dummy's clubs, leading to the ace at the third trick and ruffing a club at the fourth. The appearance of the queen from East necessitated a pause for reflection.

The routine course was to cash the heart ace and ruff a heart, continuing to cross-ruff in clubs and hearts. The clubs would eventually be established, but too late. The dummy would be entryless, and South would be left with a heart as well as a spade loser.

South foresaw the entry problem and found the solution to it. At the fifth trick he made the fine play of leading the spade queen. If the defenders took this trick, the spade king would become the extra entry needed in the dummy.

West dropped the spade eight to show an even number of cards, and East did the best he could by holding up his ace. But South was prepared for that eventuality. He cashed the heart ace and ruffed a heart. Then he led the club jack and administered the *coup de grâce* by discarding his spade five. The defenders were given a club trick instead of a spade trick, and there was still a trump in dummy to reach the club winners.

South had a well-earned eleven tricks and a score of 750 points. West looked blue, but East, as usual, was ready with words of consolation.

"It might have been worse," he announced.

"How could it be worse?" retorted his partner coldly.

"I might well have bid five spades, and they would double and get a cross-ruff going, beating me 1,100 with best defense."

Which was a rather tarnished silver lining.

NOVEMBER 11, 1973

FIVE WAYS
TO BEHAVE IN THE POSTMORTEM

Individual reaction to disaster is an area that can be effectively studied within the microcosm of the bridge table. Let us set a scene. South is playing four spades doubled, vulnerable, in a team match, and a husband-and-wife combination is defending. The male member of the partnership embarks on a line of defense that can set the contract two tricks for 500 points by routine means. Unfortunately his partner pursues a different course, is eventually endplayed, and the contract is made for a score of 790. In the postmortem the female defender claims that her defense was absolutely right and offers a technical justification that is hard to fault.

These events clearly subject the temper of the male defender to a considerable strain. The disaster is bad enough, but the failure to uncover any technical flaw in his spouse's reasoning compounds the irritation. By his subsequent behavior he can usually be classified as a member of one of four groups:

•The *Collapser* is plunged into gloom by the tragedy, loses his concentration and willpower, and plays badly for the rest of the session.

•The *Screamer* typically reacts with, "I don't care what you say. I go by results and that's a terrible result. You can do the explaining to our teammates."

•The *Bottler* stores up his comments until later that night or the next day or the next week.

•The *Saint* simply says, "Bad luck, partner. Maybe it was my fault," and continues placidly with the next hand.

And now for the case history. West opened with three hearts in the second seat, a bid that would normally be based on a seven-card suit. But as he was vulnerable he could not consider a four-heart bid with a suit lacking both ace and king.

East was intending to raise the pre-emptive opening to game but decided to postpone this action when North made a takeout double. She bid four hearts on the next round after South had bid three spades, but South promptly bid four spades, an imaginative action that turned out to be a good decision: Four hearts

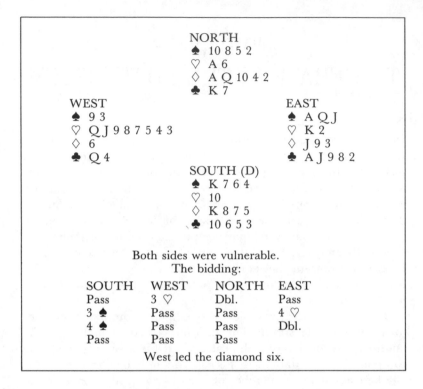

NORTH
♠ 10 8 5 2
♡ A 6
♦ A Q 10 4 2
♣ K 7

WEST
♠ 9 3
♡ Q J 9 8 7 5 4 3
♦ 6
♣ Q 4

EAST
♠ A Q J
♡ K 2
♦ J 9 3
♣ A J 9 8 2

SOUTH (D)
♠ K 7 6 4
♡ 10
♦ K 8 7 5
♣ 10 6 5 3

Both sides were vulnerable.
The bidding:

SOUTH	WEST	NORTH	EAST
Pass	3 ♡	Dbl.	Pass
3 ♠	Pass	Pass	4 ♡
4 ♠	Pass	Pass	Dbl.
Pass	Pass	Pass	

West led the diamond six.

could not have been beaten, and four spades was therefore a good save if it failed by a trick or two.

As it turned out, it did not fail at all. A club lead would have helped the defense along, but West naturally led his singleton diamond, hoping for a ruff if his partner held either the spade ace or the diamond ace. South won in dummy with the ace and led a trump. East put up the ace and started to think.

West waited in growing impatience for a diamond return, which would allow him to ruff and shift to clubs for a penalty of 500 points. He did not get it. East decided on the bidding that West probably held seven hearts and that South probably began with five spades. In that case West's distribution would be 1-4-1-7, and a diamond return for a nonexistent ruff would be fatal. South would be able to discard his heart loser on the fifth diamond and would make the hand with careful timing, whether or not he held the club queen.

So after careful reasoning East returned the heart two. The declarer was Dr. Norman Buch of New York, and he took full advantage of this reprieve. He won the heart in dummy and drew a round of trumps with the king—revealing to East the sad truth that West would have been able to ruff a diamond return.

Dummy was entered with a diamond lead to the queen, and the key play was made—a heart ruff. The position was now this:

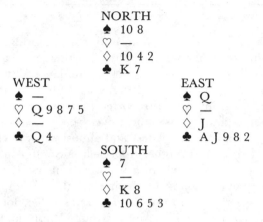

NORTH
♠ 10 8
♡ —
♢ 10 4 2
♣ K 7

WEST
♠ —
♡ Q 9 8 7 5
♢ —
♣ Q 4

EAST
♠ Q
♡ —
♢ J
♣ A J 9 8 2

SOUTH
♠ 7
♡ —
♢ K 8
♣ 10 6 5 3

South cashed the diamond king and continued the suit. There was no salvation for East. She refused to ruff, and was finally given the lead with a trump and forced to play a club. When the four players had recorded the score of 790 to North–South, she offered her well-reasoned analysis.

How did West react? He belonged to a fifth behavioral type, the *Writer,* and he simply raced to his typewriter and relieved his feelings by putting the whole sad story into print.

DECEMBER 9, 1973

TOUJOURS LA POLITESSE —UN DÉSASTRE

It is usually safe to assume, both in life and in bridge, that those around you are behaving normally. But now and again this assumption will founder on the rock of human frailty. A famous French player, Jean-Marc Roudinesco, stubbed his toe on the rock in the diagramed deal, reported by him in a book.

In a match-point game almost every partnership reached the normal contract of four spades, and almost every West doubled.

If West led some suit other than hearts, South could make his doubled game by maneuvering to discard his heart loser on the fourth round of diamonds, conceding just three trump tricks. But most Wests had the sense to lead the heart ace, followed by a heart. South ruffed and ducked a trump. West won and persevered with hearts. When South ruffed again, the position was this:

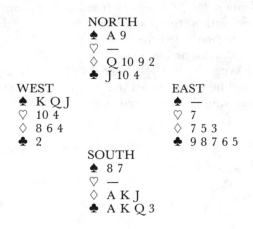

```
                NORTH
                ♠ A 9
                ♡ —
                ◇ Q 10 9 2
                ♣ J 10 4
WEST                            EAST
♠ K Q J                        ♠ —
♡ 10 4                         ♡ 7
◇ 8 6 4                        ◇ 7 5 3
♣ 2                            ♣ 9 8 7 6 5
                SOUTH
                ♠ 8 7
                ♡ —
                ◇ A K J
                ♣ A K Q 3
```

Warned by the double, the South players resigned themselves to defeat. They led clubs and forced West to ruff. That player could do no better than return the spade king, and the ace won in dummy. South announced, *"Votre atout quand vous voudrez"* (''Your trump when you wish'') and was down one.

But when Roudinesco sat South, the West player was that famous character in bridge literature: an L.O.L., little-old-lady. She was a timid L.O.L., at that, and refrained from doubling.

```
                        NORTH
                        ♠ A 9 4
                        ♡ Q 8 5
                        ◇ Q 10 9 2
                        ♣ J 10 4
        WEST                            EAST
        ♠ K Q J 10                      ♠ 2
        ♡ A 10 4 3 2                    ♡ K J 9 7
        ◇ 8 6 4                         ◇ 7 5 3
        ♣ 2                             ♣ 9 8 7 6 5
                        SOUTH (D)
                        ♠ 8 7 6 5 3
                        ♡ 6
                        ◇ A K J
                        ♣ A K Q 3
```

North and South were vulnerable.
The bidding:

SOUTH	WEST	NORTH	EAST
1 ♠	Pass	2 ♠	Pass
2 NT	Pass	3 NT	Pass
4 ♠	Dbl.	Pass	Pass
Pass			

West led the heart ace.

Now Roudinesco had no reason to suppose that the trumps would not break. Indeed, the absence of a double suggested that they would break. So in the diagramed position he led to the trump ace and was down three. At her first opportunity, West ruffed, cashed her remaining trump winner to draw the remaining trumps in the North–South hands, and took two heart tricks.

Roudinesco was in shock. For down 300 he had collected a *zéro sans partage* in his language, or an absolute bottom in ours. And he was speechless at hearing the following postmortem:

"I am afraid against you," commented the L.O.L., explaining her failure to double. "My aces disappear, as in your books, which I enjoy. Besides, you were kind enough to find a chair so that my mother could watch comfortably. I could not bring myself to profit from your misfortune and inflict a penalty of 800."

Savoring the episode to the full, there must have been an L.E.O.L., or little-even-older-lady.

MARCH 11, 1984

11

WEIRD AND WONDERFUL

W e end this collection with five oddities. The first two are bizarre psychic moves that seemed headed for disaster but turned into triumphs. In the next two the declarers survive after selecting suits in which they are outgunned by the opposition. And finally an imaginative expert changes his mind about playing in a part-score and bids a slam.

HOW TO HIDE A FREAK—WAIT

One of the most remarkable maneuvers in bidding is the striped-tail ape double. The idea is to double opponents who are on their way to a slam that will succeed before they reach it. If they meanly redouble, the doubler flees swiftly to the safety of his own suit, alternating aggression and discretion just like the anthropoid after which the double is named.

This is hardly ever attempted in practical play, although players who misjudge the auction badly be doubling them at the five-level for an overtrick sometimes brazenly claim that they intended that result. But an even more bizarre psychological coup was attempted successfully on the diagramed deal.

It was played in a rubber bridge game at the Gotham Club, 27 West 72nd Street, and the hero was the late Eddie Kayser. He was surprised to find himself with an eleven-card suit, which occurs about once in every three million deals.

The problems involved in bidding truly freakish hands such as this are psychological rather than technical. Giving information to your partner is irrelevant. What is important is to buy the contract, at almost any level, without allowing the opponents to realize the full beauty of your hand.

One theory is to bid very gently and keep bidding, letting the opponents suppose that you are simply bidding too much. On this theory South should overcall two clubs. Another idea is to lie in wait and enter the auction at a late stage, and Kayser opted for this policy.

He judged that his opponents could make a large number of tricks in their contract, and he was right about that. East can make six spades if he knows how to do it, and he would know if South has shown massive length in clubs.

The obvious move for South when his opponents reached four spades was to bid his clubs, but he felt sure that this would simply drive them to five spades. Knowing a good deal about this particular East, he made an amazing call: Double.

East could now have passed and rolled in one or two overtricks, but he liked to get every ounce of profit out of a favorable situation. As Kayser expected, he redoubled. Now West doubled the desperate retreat to five clubs, and South did not feel inclined

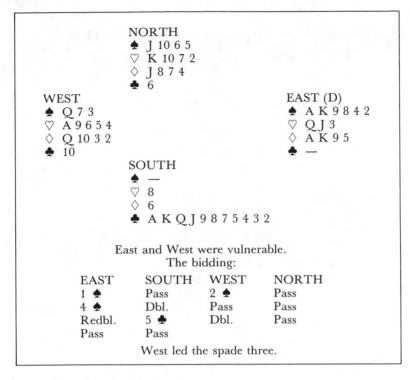

NORTH
♠ J 10 6 5
♡ K 10 7 2
◇ J 8 7 4
♣ 6

WEST
♠ Q 7 3
♡ A 9 6 5 4
◇ Q 10 3 2
♣ 10

EAST (D)
♠ A K 9 8 4 2
♡ Q J 3
◇ A K 9 5
♣ —

SOUTH
♠ —
♡ 8
◇ 6
♣ A K Q J 9 8 7 5 4 3 2

East and West were vulnerable.
The bidding:

EAST	SOUTH	WEST	NORTH
1 ♠	Pass	2 ♠	Pass
4 ♠	Dbl.	Pass	Pass
Redbl.	5 ♣	Dbl.	Pass
Pass	Pass		

West led the spade three.

to do any redoubling. He scored eleven tricks quickly, not only making a doubled game instead of his opponents doing so, but scoring one hundred honors in the bargain.

APRIL 11, 1980

A PSYCHIC TO MAKE ONE PSYCHO!

Half a century ago an aviatrix named Dorothy Rice Sims, whose main claim to bridge fame had been that she was married to P. Hal Sims, made a contribution to the game in her own right. A penchant for making outlandish bids quite unrelated to her hand, and which might on occasion deceive the opponents, led her to develop and write about the whole subject. These were at first termed psychological bids, but this was rapidly corrupted to psychic bids, something of a misnomer, or in the modern idiom, psychs.

A rash of psychic bids of every possible variety during the next quarter of a century finally convinced almost all serious tournament players that such flights of fancy should be avoided. Once the appropriate countermeasures were understood, the frequency of psychic disaster exceeded the frequency of psychic triumph. And the mere possibility of psychic maneuvering played havoc with partnership confidence.

An ethical problem also arose. If a partnership indulged in frequent psychic bids, it gained an unfair advantage. A psychic pattern inevitably developed, so that such players were more aware than the opponents that a psychic might have been made. In the upshot, only a psychic bid that led to catastrophe was free from ethical taint.

Perhaps an exception should be made on this score for the diagramed deal, where a psychic that should have resulted in disaster suddenly became the most spectacular triumph in the history of these eccentric maneuvers.

The deal was played many years ago in an international match between Holland and France. South was Bob Slavenburg, a colorful and imaginative Dutchman who some years later won the World Pairs title. He felt a psychic urge come over him when East opened one heart, so he overcalled one spade. As is usual in such bidding, he had a planned line of retreat: He would escape into clubs at the right time.

One might think that moment had come when West doubled one spade for penalties and North and East passed. But South thought he could afford to confuse the issue a little more by bidding one notrump on the way to clubs. Unfortunately this only

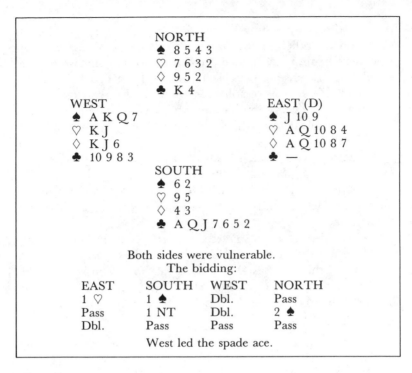

NORTH
♠ 8 5 4 3
♡ 7 6 3 2
◇ 9 5 2
♣ K 4

WEST
♠ A K Q 7
♡ K J
◇ K J 6
♣ 10 9 8 3

EAST (D)
♠ J 10 9
♡ A Q 10 8 4
◇ A Q 10 8 7
♣ —

SOUTH
♠ 6 2
♡ 9 5
◇ 4 3
♣ A Q J 7 6 5 2

Both sides were vulnerable.
The bidding:

EAST	SOUTH	WEST	NORTH
1 ♡	1 ♠	Dbl.	Pass
Pass	1 NT	Dbl.	2 ♠
Dbl.	Pass	Pass	Pass

West led the spade ace.

confused North, who now assumed that South had overcalled with a four-card spade suit and a relatively balanced hand. After West doubled again, he corrected to two spades and East doubled.

South now assumed that North would not have returned to the spade suit from which South had escaped unless he had great length and strength. So Slavenburg decided to stick it out in two spades doubled, leaving his escape suit undisclosed.

It is easy to see that two spades doubled is not an ideal contract: The defenders can take all the tricks with something to spare, scoring 2,300 points, not much more than they can collect for bidding and making the grand slam they are entitled to. But something went wrong with the defense.

A famous French expert in the West seat led the spade ace, and East dropped the jack. This irritated West, who continued with the king, not stopping to think that East must surely have the ten: He would hardly have doubled two spades holding a singleton.

East could have saved the day for the defense by playing the nine, clearly implying ownership of the ten. Instead he dropped the ten, thus augmenting West's guilt complex. The lead of the spade queen collected the nine and completed the ruin of the defenders' trumps. A shift to a red suit at this point would have enabled the defense to take eleven tricks, for a penalty of 1,700.

But West's feet were still set firmly on the road to disaster, and he played a club. South gratefully played the king from dummy, cashed the spade eight to draw the seven, and ran off clubs to make the game, scoring 670.

In the replay the Dutch East-West played in six spades, making an overtrick, and felt guilty about their failure to bid seven.

"Did the French pair reach the grand on board thirteen?" they demanded urgently when the team assembled at the end of the session.

"We made a game in spades," reported Slavenburg modestly.

"That's a different board," his teammates said impatiently. "On board thirteen East-West were cold for seven spades."

"*We* made game in spades," Slavenburg persisted, and it took half an hour to dissipate the others' incredulity.

November 5, 1972

PARTY-GOERS MAY HAVE A FIT.
OR NOT

When it opened its doors in 1967 the Essex Bridge Center in West Orange, New Jersey, was apparently the world's biggest bridge club. At the opening cocktail party the bidding and play showed occasional signs of inebriation. The winners were Judy and Gil Carroll of Livingston, New Jersey, who profited from the hair-raising proceedings on the diagramed deal.

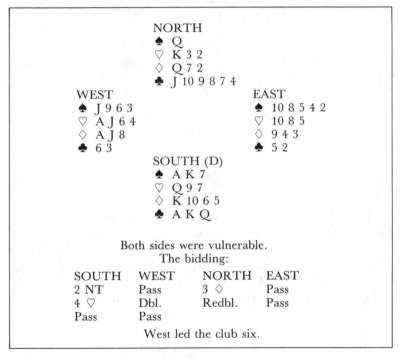

```
                    NORTH
                    ♠ Q
                    ♡ K 3 2
                    ◇ Q 7 2
                    ♣ J 10 9 8 7 4
   WEST                              EAST
   ♠ J 9 6 3                         ♠ 10 8 5 4 2
   ♡ A J 6 4                         ♡ 10 8 5
   ◇ A J 8                           ◇ 9 4 3
   ♣ 6 3                             ♣ 5 2
                    SOUTH (D)
                    ♠ A K 7
                    ♡ Q 9 7
                    ◇ K 10 6 5
                    ♣ A K Q
```

Both sides were vulnerable.
The bidding:

SOUTH	WEST	NORTH	EAST
2 NT	Pass	3 ◇	Pass
4 ♡	Dbl.	Redbl.	Pass
Pass	Pass		

West led the club six.

Carroll's bid of three diamonds in response to two notrump was an eccentric application of the Flint convention, which commands the opener to bid three hearts and usually indicates a very bad hand with a long major suit. Party-goers despise part-scores, so Mrs. Carroll violated the convention by jumping to four hearts. She thought her side could make ten tricks in her partner's presumed long major suit, a slightly optimistic assessment.

West doubled on the grounds that his opponents did not seem to know what they were doing, and North had no hesitation in redoubling. He placed his wife with heart length and was not the only one who was deceived: The defenders would have done better if they had realized that South held only three trumps.

South won the opening club lead and led a low diamond that West ducked. The queen won in dummy, and the spade queen was cashed. The closed hand was re-entered with a club, and dummy's two remaining diamonds were discarded on high spades. A diamond was ruffed, and a club lead from dummy was ruffed by East, leaving this position:

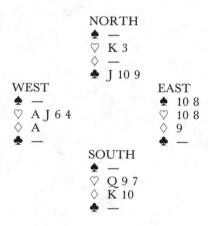

NORTH
♠ —
♡ K 3
◇ —
♣ J 10 9

WEST
♠ —
♡ A J 6 4
◇ A
♣ —

EAST
♠ 10 8
♡ 10 8
◇ 9
♣ —

SOUTH
♠ —
♡ Q 9 7
◇ K 10
♣ —

Mrs. Carroll faced an almost hopeless task in trying to make three more tricks, but her opponents were high-spirited and generous. East led a spade and South discarded a diamond. West ruffed with the heart four, with the unnecessary idea of forcing dummy's heart king. The declarer overruffed, and another club lead was ruffed and overruffed with the eight, nine, and jack.

West should have cashed the heart ace, but he could not bring himself to believe that South had started with only three hearts. He unwisely led the diamond ace, which was ruffed in dummy. South ruffed the twelfth trick with the heart seven; West overruffed with the heart ace. The heart queen gave South the last trick and a most remarkable top score.

OCTOBER 10, 1967

BLUNDERING INTO
AN UNBEATABLE CONTRACT

If one were looking for the weirdest hand of this or any year, the diagramed deal would be a good candidate. It occurred at the 1984 Summer Nationals in Washington, D.C., and was played in several events there and in some four hundred clubs throughout North America competing in the International Fund Game.

It did not seem weird, however, to the official analysts who wrote the following in advance: "The auction on this hand can start in several ways. It is normal for North to open one diamond and South to respond one spade, leaving North with a rebid problem. He can bid two notrump, even though his round-suit stoppers are weak, or he can try two clubs, hoping that South will bid again. Some will probably open one notrump to try to avoid this problem—they will, but might create another. South will probably transfer to spades, and North will lose two clubs, two spades, and probably a heart.

"If South gets very aggressive and raises spades, North will return to notrump and because of the lucky lie of the minor suits be able to take nine tricks. Those Norths who rebid two clubs after opening one diamond will fare slightly better than those languishing in two spades, since ten tricks are fairly easy. But those who play notrump will do best."

This deals with the possibility that North–South will play notrump, or spades with seven trumps, or clubs with eight trumps. One can conceive of a diamond contract with six combined trumps. A heart contract, with five trumps, would be ridiculous. But consider the auction shown in the diagram.

The names of the North–South players are not on record, and they would perhaps choose to remain anonymous. East and West, playing in the Master Mixed Team Championship, were Mark and Roberta Epstein of South Orange, New Jersey.

North, not unexpectedly, opened one notrump, and South, not unexpectedly, responded with a transfer bid of two hearts, showing spade length. West ventured a double, showing length and strength in hearts. The idea was to encourage a heart lead from East if North became the declarer.

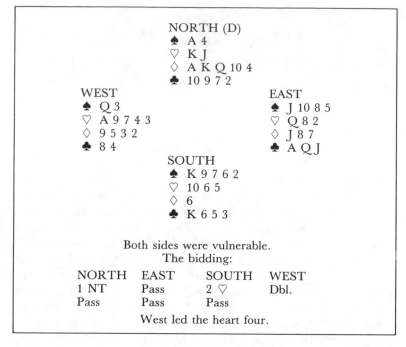

NORTH (D)
♠ A 4
♡ K J
♢ A K Q 10 4
♣ 10 9 7 2

WEST
♠ Q 3
♡ A 9 7 4 3
♢ 9 5 3 2
♣ 8 4

EAST
♠ J 10 8 5
♡ Q 8 2
♢ J 8 7
♣ A Q J

SOUTH
♠ K 9 7 6 2
♡ 10 6 5
♢ 6
♣ K 6 5 3

Both sides were vulnerable.
The bidding:

NORTH	EAST	SOUTH	WEST
1 NT	Pass	2 ♡	Dbl.
Pass	Pass	Pass	

West led the heart four.

In this somewhat unusual situation North and South proceeded to have a major confusion. North passed, intending simply to imply that he had no positive liking for spades. South apparently misunderstood and assumed that North was showing a desire to play in two hearts doubled. His pass left the partnership in an absurd contract.

In such circumstances it is usually right to lead a trump, and West did so. South had to guess immediately, and guessed wrong by playing the jack from the dummy. East won and returned a trump to the ace. West led a third round, won by South with the ten. A diamond was led, and dummy's top honors were played. When the jack fell, South was a happy man. He had five tricks, and he could not be prevented from scoring three more with the ace-king of spades and the club king. It did not matter whether he led the last diamond, forcing West to ruff, or led a club directly toward the king.

North–South scored 670 on a deal that was played in a part-score at almost all tables. East-West felt that they had been the victims of the ultimate fix.

The weird part of this is that the silly contract was unbeatable with any defense, even with a misguess at the first trick. South could not, however, have afforded a misguess in diamonds. He could have finessed the ten, playing West for a four-card suit including the jack, but that would have led to failure.

Situations of this kind are very rare in practice or theory. Jean René Vernes of France once constructed a deal in which the only makable game was four hearts with a three-two trump fit. That probably represents the ultimate.

SEPTEMBER 8, 1985

THE VALOR OF THE BETTER HALF

For two centuries the world has accepted uncritically Dr. Johnson's dictum on marriage: "A man in general is better pleased when he has a good dinner than when his wife talks Greek." Greek-speaking wives, except those who happen to come from Greece, are in even shorter supply nowadays than they were in Johnson's time. But substitute some other intellectual activity—playing bridge, for example—and the proposition becomes distinctly doubtful. In most partnerships the husband will resent a mismanaged duck much more at the bridge table than he would at the dinner table.

The marital strain is likely to be greatest when the partners are of different bridge strengths, and some husbands who are expert players have been known to go to great lengths to preserve harmony. An episode many years ago involving the diagramed deal is a case in point.

Sitting South in a duplicate game was John Lowenthal, a noted player and theorist who now lives in New York but then resided in Pittsburgh. Sitting North was his first wife, whose bridge rating was very low indeed: As declarer she usually made three or four tricks less than she had bid. On this occasion she had played several hands with uniformly disastrous results and was close to tears.

Knowing that a good score in the session was no longer possible, Lowenthal decided that he should take steps to shore up his spouse's sagging morale. The best way to do that seemed to be to arrange for her to make a contract, so when he heard a one-diamond opening opposite him he simply passed.

If one excludes players who have been barred for some legal reason, this pass may be some kind of world record: a pass of an opening bid with a hand containing 19 high-card points and five-card support for partner.

Opposite a partner who had not been able to act over one diamond, West might well have passed for the wrong reason, suspecting that North–South held an undiscovered spade fit. But he innocently balanced with one heart, an action he would later regret.

This intervention annoyed Lowenthal, who gritted his teeth

```
                    NORTH (D)
                    ♠ K Q 7 4
                    ♡ 6 2
                    ◊ A K J 4
                    ♣ 7 4 2
WEST                                    EAST
♠ —                                     ♠ J 10 9 8 5 3 2
♡ A Q 8 7 4                             ♡ 10 9 5 3
◊ 10 9                                  ◊ 6 5
♣ J 9 8 6 5 3                           ♣ —
                    SOUTH
                    ♠ A 6
                    ♡ K J
                    ◊ Q 8 7 3 2
                    ♣ A K Q 10
```

Both sides were vulnerable.
The bidding:

NORTH	EAST	SOUTH	WEST
1 ◊	Pass	Pass	1 ♡
Pass	Pass	2 ◊	Pass
Pass	2 ♡	6 NT	Pass
Pass	Pass		

West led the diamond ten.

and bid two diamonds, believing, wrongly as it happened, that his dummy would be adequate for his wife in an eight-trick contract. But when East persevered to two hearts, he had to reconsider.

Only once in a blue moon could Mrs. Lowenthal bring home nine tricks in any contract. So Lowenthal rejected a three-diamond bid, changed his objective, and thought about what he could make as declarer. The result was a dramatic leap to six notrump and a startled silence around the table.

If West had led either of his long suits, he would have given away a trick and the play would have been simple. But he led the diamond ten, giving nothing away.

South won with the ace in dummy and led a club to the ace, uncovering the break in that suit. The position was now clear to him, and as West was likely to have the heart ace, he could plan an endplay. He rapidly took one more club winner, three spade winners for a heart discard, and the remaining four diamond tricks.

His last three cards were the heart king and the queen–ten of clubs. West had been forced to keep the heart ace and the jack-nine of clubs, so he was thrown in with a heart lead and the slam was home.

Emerging from his state of shock, West had a question. Turning to the declarer, he demanded an explanation of the pass of one diamond.

"I wasn't sure my partner would be able to make more than seven tricks," was the answer.

"What do you mean by that?" asked North suspiciously.

"I was right, dear," was the soothing response. "They would have taken four ruffs and two heart tricks before you gained the lead. As it turns out, I was wrong to bid two diamonds. And as it was, I decided notrump would do pretty well."

"I'm never ever going to balance again," snarled West, who seemed close to apoplexy.

MARCH 5, 1978